Made from scratch BAKING

EVERYDAY EASY HOME COOKING

This edition published by Parragon Books Ltd in 2014
LOVE FOOD is an imprint of Parragon Books Ltd

Parragon Books Ltd
Chartist House
15–17 Trim Street
Bath BA1 1HA, UK
www.parragon.com/lovefood

ISBN 978-1-4723-2992-9

Printed in China

Cover photography by Ian Garlick
New photography by Clive Streeter
New food styling by Angela Drake and Sally Streeter
Introduction, new recipes and notes by Angela Drake
Nutritional analysis by Fiona Hunter

Notes for the Reader
This book uses both metric and imperial measurements. Follow the same
units of measurement throughout; do not mix metric and imperial. All spoon
measurements are level: teaspoons are assumed to be 5 ml, and tablespoons
are assumed to be 15 ml. Unless otherwise stated, milk is assumed to be full fat,
eggs and individual vegetables are medium, and pepper is freshly ground
black pepper. Unless otherwise stated, all root vegetables should be peeled
prior to using.

Garnishes, decorations and serving suggestions are all optional and not
necessarily included in the recipe ingredients or method. Any optional
ingredients and seasoning to taste are not included in the nutritional analysis.
The times given are an approximate guide only. Preparation times differ
according to the techniques used by different people and the cooking times
may also vary from those given. Optional ingredients, variations or serving
suggestions have not been included in the time calculations.

Contents

Introduction

There's something extra special about a home-baked cake. Whilst it may not have the perfectly proportioned features of a shop-bought version, the flavour will almost certainly be far superior and you'll also know exactly what went into it! Home baking has never been so popular...

This book is the perfect choice for novice cooks wanting to learn the basics of home baking but it's also ideal for more experienced cooks who will find a whole variety of new and original ideas to broaden their repertoire. Included are recipes ranging from cupcakes, muffins and cookies to classic cakes, tarts, breads, pies and puddings – some can easily be made in minutes, others will take longer and require a little more skill and patience.

It is worth buying good quality equipment that will last – if you like baking cupcakes then invest in a good bun tin. If you only make layer cakes occasionally, it is probably best to borrow sandwich tins from a friend. What ever you choose to bake, the finest quality ingredients will always give the best flavour.

Each recipe has clear and easy to understand numbered instructions and simple step-by-step pictures to guide you. The book is also full of useful hints and tips from freezing information to time-saving techniques and flavour variations.

Secrets of successful baking

- Prepare the kitchen before you start by clearing work surfaces and making sure you have enough space to work in.

- Check that you have all the ingredients to make the recipe – you don't want to run out of something at a crucial moment.

- Make sure that the cake tin is the correct size and prepare by greasing and/or lining.

- Preheat the oven to the required temperature and take eggs out of the refrigerator at least one hour before starting. If the recipe requires softened butter allow it to stand at room temperature for about an hour.

- For bread making, a warm kitchen will help the dough to rise so turn the oven on earlier than needed.

There is nothing more satisfying than creating delicious home-made goodies for family and friends.

- For pastry making, keep hands and equipment as cool as possible to prevent the fat from melting and making the pastry sticky.

- Always measure ingredients carefully and use measuring spoons for raising agents and flavourings.

- Don't be tempted to open the oven door too early – a rush of cold air can soon make a cake sink!

- To check if a sponge cake is ready, gently press the surface with your fingertips. It should spring back without leaving an impression. For deeper cakes or rich fruit cakes, check by inserting a skewer into the centre of the cake – it should come out clean.

- To check if bread is ready, hold the loaf with a thick tea towel and tap the base firmly with your knuckles – it should sound hollow.

- Leave cakes and bakes to cool completely before storing in airtight tins or plastic containers.

Classic Chocolate Cake *8*

Red Velvet Cake *10*

Coffee & Walnut Cake *12*

Rich Fruit Cake *14*

Pumpkin Spice Cake *16*

Coconut Layer Cake *18*

Frosted Fruits Cake *20*

Victoria Sponge Cake *22*

White Chocolate Coffee Cake *24*

Coffee Bundt Cake *26*

Angel Food Cake *28*

Mini Carrot Cakes *30*

Apple Crumb Cake *32*

Maple & Pecan Bundt Cake *34*

Cakes

Classic Chocolate Cake

 SERVES 10

 PREP TIME:
25 minutes
plus chilling

 COOKING TIME:
25–30 minutes

nutritional information per serving	581 kcals, 41g fat, 25g sat fat, 32g total sugars, 0.7g salt

For sheer indulgence, nothing beats a slice of moist chocolate cake smothered in a rich and creamy frosting.

INGREDIENTS

55 g/2 oz cocoa powder

7 tbsp boiling water

200 g/7 oz butter, softened, plus extra for greasing

125 g/4½ oz caster sugar

70 g/2½ oz soft light brown sugar

4 eggs, beaten

1 tsp vanilla extract

200 g/7 oz self-raising flour

frosting

200 g/7 oz plain chocolate, broken into pieces

115 g/4 oz unsalted butter

100 ml/3½ fl oz double cream

1. Preheat the oven to 180°C/350°F/Gas Mark 4. Grease two 20-cm/ 8-inch sandwich tins and line with baking paper.

2. Blend the cocoa powder and water to a smooth paste and set aside. Put the butter, caster sugar and brown sugar into a large bowl and beat together until pale and creamy. Gradually beat in the eggs, then stir in the cocoa paste and vanilla extract.

3. Sift in the flour and fold in gently. Divide the mixture between the prepared tins. Bake in the preheated oven for 25–30 minutes, or until risen and just springy to the touch. Leave to cool in the tins for 5 minutes, then turn out onto a wire rack to cool completely.

4. To make the frosting, put the chocolate and butter into a heatproof bowl set over a saucepan of simmering water and heat until melted. Remove from the heat and stir in the cream. Leave to cool for 20 minutes, then chill in the refrigerator for 40–50 minutes, stirring occasionally, until thick enough to spread.

5. Sandwich the sponges together with one third of the frosting, then spread the remainder over the top and sides of the cake.

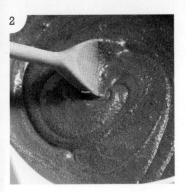

Red Velvet Cake

 SERVES 12

 PREP TIME:
25 minutes
plus cooling

 COOKING TIME:
25–30 minutes

nutritional information per serving	510 kcals, 32g fat, 20g sat fat, 28g total sugars, 0.5g salt

A popular American cake with a rich buttermilk-flavoured chocolate sponge, it is coloured deep red by edible food colouring and topped off with a traditional vanilla cream cheese frosting.

INGREDIENTS

225 g/8 oz unsalted butter, plus extra for greasing
4 tbsp water
55 g/2 oz cocoa powder
3 eggs, beaten
250 ml/9 fl oz buttermilk
2 tsp vanilla extract
2 tbsp red edible food colouring
280 g/10 oz plain flour
55 g/2 oz cornflour
1½ tsp baking powder
280 g/10 oz caster sugar

frosting
250 g/9 oz cream cheese
40 g/1½ oz unsalted butter
3 tbsp caster sugar
1 tsp vanilla extract

1. Preheat the oven to 190°C/375°F/Gas Mark 5. Grease two 23-cm/9-inch sandwich tins and line with baking paper.

2. Place the butter, water and cocoa powder in a small saucepan and heat gently, without boiling, stirring until melted and smooth. Remove from the heat and leave to cool slightly.

3. Beat together the eggs, buttermilk, vanilla extract and food colouring in a bowl until frothy. Beat in the butter mixture. Sift together the flour, cornflour and baking powder, then stir quickly and evenly into the mixture with the caster sugar.

4. Divide the mixture between the prepared tins and bake in the preheated oven for 25–30 minutes, or until risen and firm to the touch. Leave to cool in the tins for 3–4 minutes, then turn out onto a wire rack to cool completely.

5. To make the frosting, beat together all the ingredients until smooth. Use about half of the frosting to sandwich the cakes together, then spread the remainder over the top, swirling with a palette knife.

Coffee & Walnut Cake

 SERVES 8

 PREP TIME:
30 minutes
plus cooling

 COOKING TIME:
20–25 minutes

nutritional information
per serving — 667 kcals, 44g fat, 22g sat fat, 46g total sugars, 0.5g salt

Coffee and walnuts complement each other perfectly in this much-loved sandwich cake.

INGREDIENTS

175 g/6 oz unsalted butter, softened, plus extra for greasing
175 g/6 oz light muscovado sugar
3 large eggs, beaten
3 tbsp strong black coffee
175 g/6 oz self-raising flour
1½ tsp baking powder
115 g/4 oz walnut pieces
walnut halves, to decorate

frosting
115 g/4 oz unsalted butter, softened
200 g/7 oz icing sugar
1 tbsp strong black coffee
½ tsp vanilla extract

1. Preheat the oven to 180°C/350°F/Gas Mark 4. Grease two 20-cm/8-inch sandwich tins and line with baking paper.

2. Beat the butter and muscovado sugar together until pale and creamy. Gradually add the eggs, beating well after each addition. Beat in the coffee.

3. Sift the flour and baking powder into the mixture, then fold in lightly and evenly with a metal spoon. Fold in the walnut pieces. Divide the mixture between the prepared cake tins and smooth the surfaces. Bake in the preheated oven for 20–25 minutes, or until golden brown and springy to the touch. Turn out onto a wire rack to cool completely.

4. To make the frosting, beat together the butter, icing sugar, coffee and vanilla extract, mixing until smooth and creamy.

5. Use about half the mixture to sandwich the cakes together, then spread the remaining frosting on top and swirl with a palette knife. Decorate with walnut halves.

2

3

5

COOK'S NOTE
For the best
flavour, use a
strong espresso
coffee.

Rich Fruit Cake

 SERVES 16

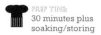 PREP TIME:
30 minutes plus
soaking/storing

 COOKING TIME:
2¼–2¾ hours

nutritional information per serving	400 kcals, 16g fat, 8.5g sat fat, 49g total sugars, 0.15g salt

The cake of choice for celebrations, such as weddings and Christmas, this classic favourite should be made well in advance to allow time for the rich flavours to mature.

INGREDIENTS

350 g/12 oz sultanas
225 g/8 oz raisins
115 g/4 oz ready-to-eat dried apricots, chopped
85 g/3 oz stoned dates, chopped
4 tbsp dark rum or brandy, plus extra for flavouring (optional)
finely grated rind and juice of 1 orange
225 g/8 oz unsalted butter, softened, plus extra for greasing
225 g/8 oz light muscovado sugar
4 eggs, beaten
70 g/2½ oz chopped mixed peel
85 g/3 oz glacé cherries, quartered
25 g/1 oz chopped glacé ginger or stem ginger
40 g/1½ oz blanched almonds, chopped
200 g/7 oz plain flour
1 tsp ground mixed spice

1. Place the sultanas, raisins, apricots and dates in a large bowl and stir in the rum, if using, orange rind and orange juice. Cover and leave to soak for several hours or overnight.

2. Preheat the oven to 150°C/300°F/Gas Mark 2. Grease a 20-cm/8-inch round deep cake tin and line with baking paper.

3. Beat the butter and sugar together until pale and creamy. Gradually beat in the eggs, beating hard after each addition. Stir in the soaked fruits, mixed peel, glacé cherries, glacé ginger and blanched almonds.

4. Sift the flour and mixed spice, then fold lightly and evenly into the mixture. Spoon the mixture into the prepared cake tin and smooth the surface, making a slight depression in the centre with the back of the spoon.

5. Bake in the preheated oven for 2¼–2¾ hours, or until the cake is beginning to shrink away from the sides and a skewer inserted into the centre comes out clean. Cool completely in the tin.

6. Turn out the cake and remove the baking paper. Wrap in some greaseproof paper and foil, and store for at least two months before use. To add a richer flavour, prick the cake with a skewer and spoon over a couple of extra tablespoons of rum or brandy, if using, before storing.

Pumpkin Spice Cake

 SERVES 8

 PREP TIME:
25 minutes
plus cooling

 COOKING TIME:
35–40 minutes

nutritional information per serving	631 kcals, 39g fat, 12g sat fat, 44g total sugars, 0.9g salt

This lightly spiced fruit and nut slab cake is smothered with a rich and creamy maple syrup frosting.

INGREDIENTS

175 ml/6 fl oz sunflower oil, plus extra for greasing
175 g/6 oz soft light brown sugar
3 eggs, beaten
250 g/9 oz canned pumpkin purée
85 g/3 oz raisins
grated rind of 1 orange
70 g/2½ oz walnut pieces
225 g/8 oz self-raising flour
1 tsp bicarbonate of soda
2 tsp mixed spice

frosting

250 g/9 oz mascarpone cheese
85 g/3 oz icing sugar
3 tbsp maple syrup

1. Preheat the oven to 180°C/350°F/Gas Mark 4. Grease a 23-cm/9-inch square cake tin and line with baking paper.

2. In a large bowl beat together the oil, brown sugar and eggs. Stir in the pumpkin purée, raisins, orange rind and 55 g/2 oz of the walnut pieces.

3. Sift together the flour, bicarbonate of soda and mixed spice and fold into the pumpkin mixture. Spoon the mixture into the prepared tin and bake in the preheated oven for 35–40 minutes, or until golden brown and firm to the touch. Leave to cool in the tin for 5 minutes, then turn out onto a wire rack to cool completely.

4. To make the frosting, put the mascarpone cheese, icing sugar and maple syrup into a bowl and beat together until smooth. Spread over the top of the cake, swirling with a palette knife. Finely chop the remaining walnut pieces and scatter over the top of the cake.

2

3

4

HEALTHY HINT
For a lighter frosting, use thick Greek-style yogurt sweetened to taste with clear honey. Spread over the cake just before serving.

Coconut Layer Cake

 SERVES 8

 PREP TIME:
30 minutes
plus cooling

 COOKING TIME:
20–25 minutes

nutritional information per serving	592 kcals, 42g fat, 26g sat fat, 28g total sugars, 0.35g salt

This cake is perfect for a special occasion with light-as-air coconut sponge filled and covered with a divinely creamy, smooth frosting.

INGREDIENTS

6 large eggs, beaten
175 g/6 oz caster sugar
175 g/6 oz plain flour
70 g/2½ oz desiccated coconut
55 g/2 oz butter, melted and cooled, plus extra for greasing
toasted coconut shavings, to decorate

frosting
250 g/9 oz mascarpone cheese
4 tbsp coconut milk
25 g/1 oz caster sugar
150 ml/5 fl oz double cream

1. Preheat the oven to 180°C/350°F/Gas Mark 4. Grease three 20-cm/8-inch round sandwich tins and line with baking paper.

2. Put the eggs and sugar into a large, heatproof bowl set over a saucepan of simmering water. Beat with an electric handheld whisk until the mixture is thick and pale and leaves a trail when the whisk is lifted.

3. Sift over half of the flour and gently fold into the whisked mixture, then sift over and fold in the rest of the flour followed by the coconut. Pour the butter in a thin stream over the mixture and fold in until just incorporated.

4. Divide the mixture between the prepared tins and bake in the preheated oven for 20–25 minutes, or until light golden and springy to the touch. Leave to cool in the tins for 5 minutes, then turn out onto a wire rack to cool completely.

5. To make the frosting, put the mascarpone cheese, coconut milk and sugar into a bowl and beat together until smooth. Whip the cream until it holds soft peaks, then fold it into the mixture.

6. Sandwich the cakes together with one third of the frosting and spread the remainder over the top and sides of the cake. Decorate with coconut shavings.

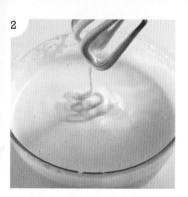

Frosted Fruits Cake

 SERVES 16   PREP TIME: 50 minutes plus chilling   COOKING TIME: 35–40 minutes

nutritional information per serving	502 kcals, 33g fat, 20g sat fat, 35g total sugars, 0.6g salt

This impressive cake is perfect for a summer afternoon tea or as a dessert after a leisurely lunch. Use firm, undamaged fruits so their juices don't seep into the frosting.

INGREDIENTS

280 g/10 oz butter, softened, plus extra for greasing
280 g/10 oz caster sugar
5 eggs, beaten
1 tbsp vanilla extract
280 g/10 oz self-raising flour
3 tbsp milk
5 tbsp raspberry or strawberry jam
150 ml/5 fl oz double cream
350–400 g/12–14 oz summer fruits, such as strawberries, raspberries and blueberries
icing sugar, for sprinkling

frosting

200 g/7 oz cream cheese
100 g/3½ oz butter, softened
1 tsp lemon juice
100 g/3½ oz icing sugar
edible pink food colouring

1. Preheat the oven to 180°C/350°F/Gas Mark 4. Grease two 20-cm/8-inch sandwich tins and line with baking paper. Put the butter and caster sugar into a bowl and beat together until pale and creamy. Gradually beat in the eggs, then stir in the vanilla extract. Sift in the flour and fold in gently. Stir in the milk. Divide the mixture between the prepared tins. Bake in the preheated oven for 35–40 minutes, or until springy to the touch. Turn out onto a wire rack to cool.

2. Place one of the cakes on a flat serving plate and spread with the jam. Whip the cream until it is just holding its shape. Spread the cream over the jam, almost to the edges of the cake. Position the second cake on top and press down gently so the cream is level with the edges of the cake.

3. To make the frosting, beat together the cream cheese and butter. Add the lemon juice and icing sugar and beat until light and creamy. Beat a dash of pink food colouring into the frosting to colour it the palest shade of pink. Using a palette knife, spread a very thin layer over the top and sides of the cake to seal in the crumbs. The cake will still show through at this stage but will be covered by the second layer of frosting. Chill in the refrigerator for 15 minutes.

4. Use the palette knife to spread a thicker layer of frosting around the sides of the cake. Spread the remainder over the top. Once evenly covered, use the edge of the palette knife to swirl the frosting as smoothly or as textured as you like. Arrange the fruits on top of the cake. Put a little icing sugar in a small, fine sieve and gently tap it over the fruits to lightly frost.

Victoria Sponge Cake

 SERVES 8

 PREP TIME:
30 minutes
plus cooling

 COOKING TIME:
25–30 minutes

nutritional information per serving	566 kcals, 42g fat, 25g sat fat, 28g total sugars, 0.8g salt

Named after Queen Victoria, this classic sandwich cake is given the star treatment with a luxurious filling of jam, softly whipped cream and fresh strawberries. Just perfect for a summer afternoon tea.

INGREDIENTS

175 g/6 oz self-raising flour
1 tsp baking powder
175 g/6 oz butter, softened, plus extra for greasing
175 g/6 oz golden caster sugar
3 eggs
icing sugar, for dusting

filling
3 tbsp raspberry jam
300 ml/10 fl oz double cream, whipped
16 fresh strawberries, halved

1. Preheat the oven to 180°C/350°F/Gas Mark 4. Grease two 20-cm/8-inch sandwich tins and line with baking paper.

2. Sift the flour and baking powder into a bowl and add the butter, sugar and eggs. Mix together, then beat well until smooth.

3. Divide the mixture evenly between the prepared tins and smooth the surfaces. Bake in the preheated oven for 25–30 minutes, or until well risen and golden brown, and the cakes feel springy when lightly pressed.

4. Leave to cool in the tins for 5 minutes, then turn out and peel off the baking paper. Transfer to wire racks to cool completely. Sandwich the cakes together with the raspberry jam, whipped double cream and strawberry halves. Dust with icing sugar.

2

3

4

COOK'S NOTE
To create a lacy pattern, place a doily over the cake and dust with icing sugar.

White Chocolate Coffee Cake

 SERVES 10

 PREP TIME: 30 minutes plus chilling

 COOKING TIME: 25–30 minutes

nutritional information per serving	467 kcals, 27g fat, 16g sat fat, 40g total sugars, 0.2g salt

This coffee-flavoured sponge has a wonderful smooth and tangy crème fraîche and white chocolate icing.

INGREDIENTS

40 g/1½ oz unsalted butter, plus extra for greasing
85 g/3 oz white chocolate, broken into pieces
125 g/4½ oz caster sugar
4 large eggs, beaten
2 tbsp very strong black coffee
1 tsp vanilla extract
125 g/4½ oz plain flour

icing
175 g/6 oz white chocolate
85 g/3 oz unsalted butter
125 g/4½ oz crème fraîche
125 g/4½ oz icing sugar, sifted
1 tbsp coffee liqueur

1. Preheat the oven to 180°C/350°F/Gas Mark 4. Grease two 20-cm/8-inch sandwich tins and line with baking paper. Place the butter and chocolate in a heatproof bowl set over a saucepan of gently simmering water and heat until melted. Stir to mix, then remove from the heat. Place the caster sugar, eggs, coffee and vanilla extract in a bowl set over a saucepan of hot water and whisk until it leaves a trail when the whisk is lifted. Remove from the heat, sift in the flour and mix in lightly and evenly. Quickly stir in the butter and chocolate mixture, then divide the mixture between the prepared tins. Bake in the preheated oven for 25–30 minutes, until risen, golden brown and springy to the touch. Leave to cool in the tins for 2 minutes, then turn out onto a wire rack.

2. To make the icing, place the chocolate and butter in a bowl set over a saucepan of hot water and heat gently until melted. Remove from the heat, stir in the crème fraîche, then add the icing sugar and coffee liqueur and mix. Chill the icing until thick. Use one third of the icing to sandwich the cake together, then spread the rest over the cake.

Coffee Bundt Cake

 SERVES 14

 PREP TIME:
40 minutes
plus cooling

 COOKING TIME:
50 minutes

nutritional information per serving	505 kcals, 28g fat, 17g sat fat, 36g total sugars, 0.9g salt

Bundt cakes cook quickly and, therefore, stay deliciously moist due to the hole through the centre of the tin.

INGREDIENTS

400 g/14 oz plain flour, plus extra for dusting
1 tbsp baking powder
1 tsp bicarbonate of soda
3 tbsp espresso coffee powder
275 g/9¾ oz lightly salted butter, softened, plus extra for greasing
125 g/4½ oz light muscovado sugar
225 ml/8 fl oz maple syrup
3 eggs, beaten
225 ml/8 fl oz buttermilk
225 ml/8 fl oz double cream

decoration
4 tbsp maple syrup
200 g/7 oz icing sugar
15 g/½ oz unsalted butter, melted
20 chocolate-coated coffee beans

1. Preheat the oven to 180°C/350°F/Gas Mark 4. Grease and lightly flour a 3-litre/5¼-pint Bundt tin.

2. Sift the flour, baking powder, bicarbonate of soda and coffee powder into a bowl. In a separate bowl, beat together the butter and muscovado sugar until pale and creamy. Gradually whisk in the maple syrup. Beat in the eggs slowly, adding 3 tablespoons of the flour mixture to prevent curdling.

3. Mix together the buttermilk and cream and add half to the butter mixture. Sprinkle in half of the flour mixture and fold gently together. Add the remaining buttermilk and flour mixtures and mix together gently until just combined.

4. Spoon the mixture into the prepared tin and smooth the surface. Bake in the preheated oven for about 50 minutes, or until well risen and a skewer inserted into the centre comes out clean. Leave in the tin for 10 minutes, then loosen with a knife and turn out onto a wire rack to cool completely.

5. To decorate, beat the maple syrup in a bowl with 150 g/5½ oz of the icing sugar and the butter, until smooth and thickly coating the back of a wooden spoon. Transfer the cake to a serving plate and spoon the icing around the top of the cake so it starts to run down the sides.

6. Beat the remaining icing sugar in a small bowl with 1½–2 teaspoons of water to make a smooth paste. Using a teaspoon, drizzle the icing over the cake. Scatter the coffee beans over the top.

Angel Food Cake

 SERVES 10

 PREP TIME:
30 minutes
plus cooling

 COOKING TIME:
40–45 minutes

nutritional information per serving	171 kcals, 0.5g fat, 0.1g sat fat, 29g total sugars, 0.13g salt

This light fat-free whisked sponge is topped with fresh berries and makes a great dessert for a summer barbecue or al fresco meal.

INGREDIENTS

sunflower oil, for greasing
8 large egg whites
1 tsp cream of tartar
1 tsp almond extract
250 g/9 oz caster sugar
115 g/4 oz plain flour,
plus extra for dusting

decoration
250 g/9 oz summer berries
1 tbsp lemon juice
2 tbsp icing sugar

1. Preheat the oven to 160°C/325°F/Gas Mark 3. Grease and lightly flour a 24-cm/9½-inch ring tin.

2. In a clean, grease-free bowl, whisk the egg whites until they hold soft peaks. Add the cream of tartar and whisk again until the whites are stiff but not dry. Whisk in the almond extract, then add the caster sugar, a tablespoon at a time, whisking hard between each addition. Sift in the flour and fold in lightly and evenly using a large metal spoon.

3. Spoon the mixture into the prepared cake tin. Bake in the preheated oven for 40–45 minutes, or until golden brown. Run the tip of a knife around the edges of the cake to loosen from the tin. Leave to cool in the tin for 10 minutes, then turn out onto a wire rack to cool.

4. To decorate, place the berries, lemon juice and icing sugar in a saucepan and heat until the sugar has dissolved. Spoon over the cake.

2

2

3

GOES WELL WITH
Serve this delicious cake with whipped double cream sweetened with a little icing sugar.

Mini Carrot Cakes

 MAKES 20

 PREP TIME:
1 hour
plus cooling

 COOKING TIME:
35 minutes

nutritional information per cake	250 kcals, 15.5g fat, 8g sat fat, 19g total sugars, 0.32g salt

Carrot cake is such an all-time favourite, it quite simply had to be included here. If you're making these in advance, the little marzipan carrots can be positioned after frosting the cake.

INGREDIENTS

150 g/5½ oz lightly salted butter, softened, plus extra for greasing

150 g/5½ oz light muscovado sugar

3 eggs, beaten

150 g/5½ oz self-raising flour

½ tsp baking powder

½ tsp ground mixed spice

85 g/3 oz ground almonds

finely grated rind of 1 lemon

150 g/5½ oz carrots, grated

85 g/3 oz sultanas, roughly chopped

decoration

150 g/5½ oz full-fat cream cheese

40 g/1½ oz unsalted butter, softened

115 g/4 oz icing sugar, plus extra for dusting

2 tbsp lemon juice

60 g/2¼ oz marzipan

edible orange food colouring

several sprigs of dill

1. Preheat the oven to 180°C/350°F/Gas Mark 4. Grease a 25-cm x 20-cm/10-inch x 8-inch roasting tin or similar sized tin and line with baking paper. Grease the baking paper. Put the butter, light muscovado sugar, eggs, flour, baking powder, mixed spice, almonds and lemon rind in a mixing bowl and beat together with an electric handheld whisk until smooth and creamy. Stir in the carrots and sultanas.

2. Spoon the mixture into the prepared tin and smooth the surface. Bake in the preheated oven for 35 minutes, or until risen and just firm to the touch. Leave in the tin for 10 minutes, then transfer to a wire rack to cool.

3. For the decoration, beat together the cream cheese, butter, icing sugar and lemon juice until creamy. Colour the marzipan deep orange by dotting a few drops of the food colouring onto the marzipan and rolling out the marzipan on a surface lightly dusted with icing sugar, rolling until the colour is evenly mixed. Roll the marzipan into a sausage shape then divide it into 20 pieces and form each one into a small carrot shape, marking shallow grooves around each with a knife.

4. Using a palette knife, spread the frosting over the cake, taking it almost to the edges. Trim the crusts from the cake to neaten it, then cut it into 20 squares. Place a marzipan carrot on each cake and add a small sprig of dill.

Apple Crumb Cake

 SERVES 10

 PREP TIME:
30 minutes
plus chilling

 COOKING TIME:
1 hour, 20 mins

nutritional information per serving	451 kcals, 26g fat, 13g sat fat, 28g total sugars, 0.7g salt

Chunks of moist apple in a spiced sponge, topped off with a deliciously nutty crumb crust – irresistible!

INGREDIENTS

175 g/6 oz butter, softened, plus extra for greasing
175 g/6 oz caster sugar
3 large eggs, beaten
2 tbsp milk
225 g/8 oz self-raising flour
1 tsp ground cinnamon
½ tsp grated nutmeg
2 cooking apples, peeled, cored and chopped (500 g/1 lb 2 oz unpeeled weight)
clotted cream, to serve

crumb topping
85 g/3 oz self-raising flour
55 g/2 oz butter, chilled and diced
55 g/2 oz demerara sugar
55 g/2 oz blanched hazelnuts, chopped

1. Preheat the oven to 180°C/350°F/Gas Mark 4. Grease a 23-cm/9-inch round springform cake tin and line with baking paper.

2. Put the butter and caster sugar into a large bowl and beat together until pale and fluffy, then gradually beat in the eggs. Stir in the milk. Sift together the flour and spices and gently fold in until thoroughly incorporated.

3. Spoon half the mixture into the prepared tin and scatter over half the apples. Spoon over the remaining mixture and spread evenly. Top with the remaining apples.

4. To make the crumb topping, sift the flour into a bowl, then add the butter and rub in until the mixture resembles breadcrumbs. Stir in the demerara sugar and nuts. Sprinkle the mixture evenly over the cake.

5. Bake in the preheated oven for 1 hour, then cover loosely with foil to prevent over-browning. Cook for a further 10–20 minutes, or until golden brown and firm to the touch. Leave to cool in the tin for 20 minutes, then unclip the tin and carefully transfer to a wire rack. Serve warm or cold, with clotted cream.

Maple & Pecan Bundt Cake

 SERVES 10   PREP TIME: 30 minutes plus cooling   COOKING TIME: 45–50 minutes

nutritional information per serving	466 kcals, 28g fat, 14g sat fat, 33g total sugars, 0.6g salt

Baked in a classic fluted Bundt tin, this cake looks and tastes amazing.

INGREDIENTS

200 g/7 oz butter, softened, plus extra for greasing

200 g/7 oz soft light brown sugar

3 large eggs, beaten

55 g/2 oz pecan nuts, very finely chopped

4 tbsp maple syrup

150 ml/5 fl oz soured cream

225 g/8 oz self-raising flour, plus extra for dusting

chopped pecan nuts, to decorate

icing

85 g/3 oz icing sugar, sifted

1 tbsp maple syrup

1–2 tbsp lukewarm water

1. Preheat the oven to 160°C/325°F/Gas Mark 3. Grease and lightly flour a 2-litre/3½-pint Bundt tin.

2. Put the butter and brown sugar into a bowl and beat together until pale and fluffy. Gradually beat in the eggs, then stir in the nuts, maple syrup and soured cream. Sift in the flour and fold in thoroughly.

3. Spoon the mixture into the prepared tin and gently smooth the surface. Bake in the preheated oven for 45–50 minutes, or until the cake is firm and golden and a skewer inserted into the centre comes out clean. Leave to cool in the tin for 10 minutes, then turn out onto a wire rack to cool completely.

4. To make the icing, mix the icing sugar, maple syrup and enough water to make a smooth icing. Spoon the icing over the top of the cake, allowing it to run down the sides. Decorate with the chopped nuts and leave to set.

2

3

3

COOK'S NOTE
Before turning the cake out of the tin, gently loosen the edges from the sides with the tip of a thin spatula.

Classic Vanilla Cupcakes *38*

Berry Muffins *40*

White Chocolate & Raspberry Muffins *42*

Ultimate Chocolate Cupcakes *44*

Chocolate Chip Muffins *46*

Frosted Berry Cupcakes *48*

Hummingbird Cupcakes *50*

Chocolate & Orange Muffins *52*

Apple & Cinnamon Muffins *54*

Tiramisù Cupcakes *56*

Blueberry Muffins *58*

Candy Cupcakes *60*

Fudge Nut Muffins *62*

Apple Streusel Cupcakes *64*

Cupcakes & Muffins

Classic Vanilla Cupcakes

 MAKES 12

 PREP TIME: 25 minutes

 COOKING TIME: 15–20 minutes

nutritional information per cupcake — 453 kcals, 27g fat, 17g sat fat, 40g total sugars, 0.2g salt

Everyone's favourite – light and fluffy vanilla sponges topped with generous swirls of buttercream frosting.

INGREDIENTS

175 g/6 oz unsalted butter, softened
175 g/6 oz caster sugar
3 large eggs, beaten
1 tsp vanilla extract
175 g/6 oz self-raising flour

frosting
150 g/5½ oz unsalted butter, softened
3 tbsp double cream or milk
1 tsp vanilla extract
300 g/10½ oz icing sugar, sifted
hundreds and thousands, to decorate

1. Preheat the oven to 180°C/350°F/Gas Mark 4. Place 12 paper cases in a muffin tin.

2. Put the butter and caster sugar into a bowl and beat together until pale and creamy. Gradually beat in the eggs and vanilla extract. Sift in the flour and fold in gently.

3. Divide the mixture evenly between the paper cases and bake in the preheated oven for 15–20 minutes, or until risen and firm to the touch. Transfer to a wire rack and leave to cool.

4. To make the frosting, put the butter into a bowl and beat with an electric mixer for 2–3 minutes, or until pale and creamy. Beat in the cream and vanilla extract. Gradually beat in the icing sugar and continue beating until the buttercream is light and fluffy.

5. Use a palette knife to swirl the frosting over the tops of the cupcakes. Decorate with hundreds and thousands.

2

3

5

SOMETHING DIFFERENT

To make bite-sized cupcakes for children's parties, divide the mixture between 30 mini muffin cases and reduce the cooking time to 8-10 minutes.

Berry Muffins

 MAKES 12

 PREP TIME:
20 minutes

 COOKING TIME:
20–25 minutes

nutritional information
per muffin
255 kcals, 15g fat, 7g sat fat, 13g total sugars, 0.5g salt

*Quick and easy to make, these muffins are packed full
of fresh summer berries.*

INGREDIENTS

225 g/8 oz plain flour

2 tsp baking powder

55 g/2 oz ground almonds

125 g/4½ oz caster sugar,
plus extra for sprinkling

150 g/5½ oz butter, melted

100 ml/3½ fl oz milk

2 eggs, beaten

250 g/9 oz mixed berries, such
as blueberries, raspberries,
blackberries and redcurrants

1. Preheat the oven to 190°C/375°F/Gas Mark 5. Place 12 paper cases in a muffin tin.

2. Sift together the flour and baking powder into a large bowl and stir in the ground almonds and sugar. Make a well in the centre of the dry ingredients.

3. Beat together the butter, milk and eggs and pour into the well. Stir gently until just combined; do not over-mix. Gently fold in the berries.

4. Divide the mixture evenly between the paper cases. Bake in the preheated oven for 20–25 minutes, or until light golden and just firm to the touch. Serve warm or cold, sprinkled with sugar.

FREEZING TIP
The cold muffins
will freeze for
up to 2 months.
Thaw at room
temperature for
1-2 hours.

White Chocolate & Raspberry Muffins

 MAKES 12

 PREP TIME
20 minutes

 COOKING TIME
20–25 minutes

nutritional information per muffin	246 kcals, 11g fat, 6.5g sat fat, 18g total sugars, 0.5g salt

Best eaten warm from the oven, these muffins make a great mid-morning snack.

INGREDIENTS

250 g/9 oz plain flour
1 tbsp baking powder
115 g/4 oz caster sugar
85 g/3 oz butter, chilled and roughly grated
1 large egg, beaten
175 ml/6 fl oz milk
175 g/6 oz raspberries
140 g/5 oz white chocolate chips

1. Preheat the oven to 200°C/400°F/Gas Mark 6. Place 12 paper cases in a muffin tin.

2. Sift together the flour and baking powder into a large bowl and stir in the sugar. Add the butter and stir with a fork to coat in the flour mixture. Lightly beat the egg in a jug or bowl, then beat in the milk.

3. Make a well in the centre of the dry ingredients and pour in the beaten liquid ingredients. Stir gently until just combined; do not over-mix. Fold in the raspberries and half of the chocolate chips.

4. Divide the mixture evenly between the paper cases and scatter over the remaining chocolate chips. Bake in the preheated oven for 20–25 minutes, or until risen, golden and just firm to the touch. Leave to cool for 5 minutes, then transfer to a wire rack to cool completely.

2

3

4

SOMETHING DIFFERENT

Replace the raspberries with fresh or frozen blackberries, or try chopped fresh mango for a tropical flavour.

Ultimate Chocolate Cupcakes

 MAKES 14

 PREP TIME:
25 minutes
plus chilling

 COOKING TIME:
15–20 minutes

nutritional information per cupcake	440 kcals, 28g fat, 17g sat fat, 37g total sugars, 0.33g salt

Moist chocolate sponges topped with large swirls of rich and creamy frosting – these cupcakes are simply the best! Ideal for a special celebration or birthday as they can be made a day in advance.

INGREDIENTS

115 g/4 oz self-raising flour
½ tsp baking powder
1½ tbsp cocoa powder
115 g/4 oz butter, softened, or soft margarine
115 g/4 oz caster sugar
2 large eggs, beaten
55 g/2 oz plain chocolate, melted

frosting
150 g/5½ oz plain chocolate, finely chopped
200 ml/7 fl oz double cream
140 g/5 oz unsalted butter, softened
280 g/10 oz icing sugar, sifted
chocolate shapes and gold dragées, to decorate (optional)

1. Preheat the oven to 180°C/350°F/Gas Mark 4. Place 14 paper cases in a bun tin.

2. Sift the flour, baking powder and cocoa powder into a large bowl. Add the butter, caster sugar and eggs and beat together until smooth. Fold in the melted chocolate.

3. Divide the mixture evenly between the paper cases. Bake in the preheated oven for 15–20 minutes, or until risen and firm to the touch. Transfer to a wire rack and leave to cool.

4. To make the frosting, put the chocolate in a heatproof bowl. Heat the cream in a saucepan until boiling, then pour over the chocolate and stir until smooth. Leave to cool for 20 minutes, stirring occasionally, until thickened. Put the butter in a bowl, stir in the icing sugar and beat until smooth. Beat in the chocolate mixture. Chill for 15–20 minutes.

5. Spoon the frosting into a piping bag fitted with a large star nozzle. Pipe swirls of frosting on top of each cupcake. Decorate with chocolate shapes and gold dragées, if using.

Chocolate Chip Muffins

 MAKES 12   PREP TIME: 20 minutes   COOKING TIME 20–25 minutes

nutritional information
per muffin   252 kcals, 11g fat, 6.5g sat fat, 18g total sugars, 0.6g salt

These classic American muffins have a lovely light texture and are full of delicious milk chocolate chunks.

INGREDIENTS

300 g/10½ oz self-raising flour
1½ tsp baking powder
85 g/3 oz butter, chilled and diced
85 g/3 oz caster sugar
150 g/5½ oz milk chocolate, chopped into chunks
2 large eggs, beaten
200 ml/7 fl oz buttermilk
1 tsp vanilla extract

1. Preheat the oven to 200°C/400°F/Gas Mark 6. Place 12 paper cases in a muffin tin.

2. Sift together the flour and baking powder into a large bowl. Add the butter and rub in to make fine breadcrumbs. Stir in the sugar and the chocolate chunks.

3. Beat together the eggs, buttermilk and vanilla extract. Make a well in the centre of the dry ingredients and pour in the beaten liquid ingredients. Stir gently until just combined; do not over-mix.

4. Divide the mixture evenly between the paper cases. Bake in the preheated oven for 20–25 minutes, or until risen, golden and just firm to the touch. Leave to cool for 5 minutes, then transfer to a wire rack to cool completely.

2

2

4

COOK'S NOTE

To make your own muffin cases, cut out 13-cm/5-inch squares of baking paper. Press into the tin, smoothing down the folds.

Frosted Berry Cupcakes

 MAKES 12   PREP TIME 25 minutes   COOKING TIME 15–20 minutes

nutritional information per cupcake	330 kcals, 22.5g fat, 12.5g sat fat, 21g total sugars, 0.3g salt

These summer cupcakes are scented with orange flower water and topped with a creamy mascarpone frosting.

INGREDIENTS

115 g/4 oz butter, softened, or soft margarine
115 g/4 oz caster sugar
2 tsp orange flower water
2 large eggs, beaten
55 g/2 oz ground almonds
115 g/4 oz self-raising flour
2 tbsp milk

frosting
300 g/10½ oz mascarpone cheese
85 g/3 oz caster sugar
4 tbsp orange juice

decoration
280 g/10 oz berries, fresh mint leaves, egg white and sugar

1. Preheat the oven to 180°C/350°F/Gas Mark 4. Place 12 paper cases in a bun tin.

2. Place the butter, caster sugar and orange flower water in a large bowl and beat together until light and fluffy. Gradually beat in the eggs. Stir in the ground almonds. Sift in the flour and, using a metal spoon, fold in gently with the milk.

3. Divide the mixture evenly between the paper cases. Bake in the preheated oven for 15–20 minutes, or until risen, golden and firm to the touch. Transfer to a wire rack and leave to cool.

4. To make the frosting, put the mascarpone, caster sugar and orange juice in a bowl and beat together until smooth.

5. Swirl the frosting over the top of the cupcakes. Brush the berries and mint leaves with egg white and roll in the sugar to coat. Decorate the cupcakes with the frosted berries and leaves.

2

5

5

COOK'S NOTE
To lightly frost the
berries, brush gently
with beaten egg white
then dust with
caster sugar.

Hummingbird Cupcakes

 MAKES 12

 PREP TIME: 25 minutes

 COOKING TIME: 15–20 minutes

nutritional information per cupcake | 150 kcals, 20g fat, 8g sat fat, 36g total sugars, 0.4g salt

These delicious cupcakes are packed with pineapple, banana and pecan nuts, and lightly spiced with cinnamon. Decorated with a rich and creamy soft cheese frosting, they are as sweet as nectar!

INGREDIENTS

150 g/5½ plain flour
¾ tsp bicarbonate of soda
1 tsp ground cinnamon
125 g/4½ oz soft light brown sugar
2 eggs, beaten
100 ml/3½ fl oz sunflower oil
1 ripe banana (about 85 g/3 oz peeled weight), mashed
2 canned pineapple rings, drained and finely chopped
25 g/1 oz pecan nuts, finely chopped, plus extra sliced pecan nuts to decorate

frosting
140 g/5 oz full-fat soft cheese
70 g/2½ oz unsalted butter, softened
1 tsp vanilla extract
280 g/10 oz icing sugar, sifted

1. Preheat the oven to 180°C/350°F/Gas Mark 4. Place 12 paper cases in a bun tin.

2. Sift the flour, bicarbonate of soda and cinnamon into a bowl and stir in the sugar. Add the eggs, oil, banana, pineapple and chopped pecan nuts and mix thoroughly. Divide the mixture evenly between the paper cases.

3. Bake the cupcakes in the preheated oven for 15–20 minutes, or until risen, golden and firm to the touch. Transfer to a wire rack and leave to cool.

4. To make the frosting, put the soft cheese, butter and vanilla extract in a bowl and blend together with a spatula. Beat in the icing sugar until smooth and creamy. Pipe or swirl the frosting on the top of the cupcakes. Decorate with sliced pecan nuts.

Chocolate & Orange Muffins

 MAKES 12

 PREP TIME
20 minutes
plus cooling

 COOKING TIME
20 minutes

nutritional information per muffin	408 kcals, 21g fat, 9.5g sat fat, 37g total sugars, 0.8g salt

These sweet and crumbly muffins are full of chocolate chips and flavoured with tangy orange zest and juice. To make them even more delicious, they have a rich chocolate buttercream topping.

INGREDIENTS

2 oranges
about 125 ml/4 fl oz milk
225 g/8 oz plain flour
55 g/2 oz cocoa powder
1 tbsp baking powder
pinch of salt
115 g/4 oz soft light brown sugar
150 g/5½ oz plain chocolate chips
2 eggs
6 tbsp sunflower oil or 85 g/3 oz butter, melted and cooled
strips of orange zest, to decorate

icing

55 g/2 oz plain chocolate, broken into pieces
25 g/1 oz butter
2 tbsp water
175 g/6 oz icing sugar

1. Preheat the oven to 200°C/400°F/Gas Mark 6. Place 12 paper cases in a muffin tin.

2. Finely grate the rind from the oranges and squeeze the juice. Add enough milk to make up the juice to 250 ml/9 fl oz, then add the orange rind. Sift together the flour, cocoa powder, baking powder and salt into a large bowl. Stir in the brown sugar and chocolate chips. Place the eggs in a large jug or bowl and beat lightly, then beat in the milk and orange mixture and the oil. Make a well in the centre of the dry ingredients and pour in the beaten liquid ingredients. Stir gently until just combined; do not over-mix. Divide the mixture evenly between the paper cases.

3. Bake in the preheated oven for 20 minutes, or until well risen and firm to the touch. Leave to cool in the tin for 5 minutes, then transfer to a wire rack to cool completely.

4. To make the icing, place the chocolate in a heatproof bowl, add the butter and water, then set the bowl over a saucepan of gently simmering water and heat, stirring, until melted. Remove from the heat and sift in the icing sugar. Beat until smooth, then spread the icing on top of the muffins and decorate with strips of orange zest.

Apple & Cinnamon Muffins

 MAKES 12

PREP TIME:
20 minutes

COOKING TIME:
20–25 minutes

nutritional information
per muffin

210 kcals, 9g fat, 2g sat fat, 13g total sugars, 0.3g salt

Wholesome muffins made with oatmeal, brown sugar and grated apple - delicious warm from the oven.

INGREDIENTS

200 g/7 oz wholemeal plain flour
75 g/2¾ oz fine oatmeal
2 tsp baking powder
1 tsp ground cinnamon
125 g/4½ oz soft light brown sugar
2 large eggs
225 ml/8 fl oz semi-skimmed milk
100 ml/3½ fl oz groundnut oil
1 tsp vanilla extract
1 large cooking apple, peeled, cored and grated

1. Preheat the oven to 180°C/350°F/Gas Mark 4. Place 12 paper cases in a muffin tin.

2. Sift together the flour, oatmeal, baking powder and cinnamon into a large bowl, adding any husks that remain in the sieve. Stir in the sugar.

3. Lightly beat the eggs in a large jug, then beat in the milk, oil and vanilla extract. Make a well in the centre of the dry ingredients and pour in the beaten liquid ingredients. Stir gently until just combined; do not over-mix. Stir in the apple.

4. Divide the mixture evenly between the paper cases. Bake in the preheated oven for 20–25 minutes, or until well risen, golden brown and firm to the touch.

5. Leave the muffins in the tin for 5 minutes, then serve warm or transfer to a wire rack and leave to cool.

2

3

3

Tiramisù Cupcakes

 MAKES 12

 PREP TIME:
25 minutes
plus cooling

 COOKING TIME:
15–20 minutes

nutritional information
per cupcake | 284 kcals, 18g fat, 11g sat fat, 21g total sugars, 0.2g salt

These scrumptious cupcakes are like the classic Italian dessert - coffee, creamy mascarpone and Marsala wine.

INGREDIENTS

115 g/4 oz unsalted butter, softened
115 g/4 oz soft light brown sugar
2 eggs, beaten
115 g/4 oz self-raising flour, sifted
½ tsp baking powder
2 tsp coffee granules
25 g/1 oz icing sugar
4 tbsp water
2 tbsp finely grated plain chocolate, for dusting

frosting
225 g/8 oz mascarpone cheese
85 g/3 oz caster sugar
2 tbsp Marsala or sweet sherry

1. Preheat the oven to 180°C/350°F/Gas Mark 4. Place 12 paper cases in a bun tin.

2. Place the butter, brown sugar, eggs, flour and baking powder in a bowl and beat together until pale and creamy. Divide the mixture evenly between the paper cases.

3. Bake the cupcakes in the preheated oven for 15–20 minutes, or until risen, golden and firm to the touch.

4. Place the coffee granules, icing sugar and water in a saucepan and heat gently, stirring, until the coffee and sugar have dissolved. Boil for 1 minute then leave to cool for 10 minutes. Brush the coffee syrup over the top of the warm cupcakes. Transfer the cupcakes to a wire rack and leave to cool.

5. For the frosting, put the mascarpone, sugar and Marsala in a bowl and beat together until smooth. Spread over the top of the cakes. Using a star template, sprinkle the grated chocolate over the frosting.

2

4

5

BE PREPARED
The flavour of the cupcakes will improve if they are made a day in advance. Decorate just before serving.

Blueberry Muffins

 MAKES 12

 PREP TIME
20 minutes

 COOKING TIME
20 minutes

nutritional information
per muffin

200 kcals, 8g fat, 1.5g sat fat, 12g total sugars, 0.5g salt

Dotted with juicy blueberries and flavoured with lemon and vanilla, these buttery muffins will be snapped up as soon as they come out of the oven.

INGREDIENTS

280 g/10 oz plain flour
1 tbsp baking powder
pinch of salt
115 g/4 oz soft light brown sugar
150 g/5½ oz frozen blueberries
2 eggs
250 ml/9 fl oz milk
85 g/3 oz butter, melted and cooled
1 tsp vanilla extract
finely grated rind of 1 lemon

1. Preheat the oven to 200°C/400°F/Gas Mark 6. Place 12 paper cases in a muffin tin. Sift together the flour, baking powder and salt into a large bowl. Stir in the sugar and blueberries.

2. Lightly beat the eggs in a large jug, then beat in the milk, melted butter, vanilla extract and lemon rind. Make a well in the centre of the dry ingredients and pour in the beaten liquid ingredients. Stir gently until just combined; do not over-mix.

3. Divide the mixture evenly between the paper cases. Bake in the preheated oven for about 20 minutes, or until well risen, golden brown and firm to the touch.

4. Leave the muffins in the tin for 5 minutes, then serve warm or transfer to a wire rack and leave to cool.

1

2

3

Candy Cupcakes

 MAKES 12

 PREP TIME:
25 minutes
plus cooling

 COOKING TIME:
18–22 minutes

nutritional information per cupcake	435 kcals, 24g fat, 15g sat fat, 42g total sugars, 0.4g salt

These fun cupcakes will make a great treat for children's birthday parties. Why not let them have a go at decorating the cakes themselves? Just make sure you have lots of sweets!

INGREDIENTS

150 g/5½ oz butter, softened, or soft margarine
150 g/5½ oz caster sugar
3 eggs, beaten
150 g/5½ oz self-raising flour
4 tsp strawberry-flavoured popping candy
sweets of your choice, to decorate (optional)

buttercream
175 g/6 oz unsalted butter, softened
2 tbsp milk
350 g/12 oz icing sugar
edible pink and yellow food colourings

1. Preheat the oven to 180°C/350°F/Gas Mark 4. Place 12 paper cases in a bun tin.

2. Place the butter and caster sugar in a large bowl and beat together until pale and creamy. Gradually beat in the eggs. Sift in the flour and, using a metal spoon, fold in gently. Fold in half of the popping candy.

3. Divide the mixture evenly between the paper cases. Bake in the preheated oven for 18–22 minutes, or until risen, golden and firm to the touch. Transfer to a wire rack and leave to cool.

4. To make the buttercream, place the butter in a bowl and beat until pale and creamy. Beat in the milk, then gradually sift in the icing sugar and continue beating for 2–3 minutes, or until the buttercream is light and fluffy. Divide the buttercream between two bowls and beat a little pink or yellow food colouring into each bowl.

5. Pipe or swirl the buttercream on top of the cupcakes and decorate with sweets, if using. Sprinkle over the remaining popping candy just before serving.

3

5

5

Fudge Nut Muffins

 MAKES 12

 PREP TIME:
20 minutes

 COOKING TIME:
20–25 minutes

nutritional information
per muffin   280 kcals, 13g fat, 5g sat fat, 18g total sugars, 0.6g salt

Peanut butter gives these muffins a wonderful nutty flavour and a lovely crunchy texture.

INGREDIENTS

250 g/9 oz plain flour
4 tsp baking powder
85 g/3 oz caster sugar
6 tbsp crunchy peanut butter
1 large egg
175 ml/6 fl oz milk
55 g/2 oz butter, melted
and cooled
150 g/5½ oz vanilla fudge,
cut into small pieces
3 tbsp roughly chopped
unsalted peanuts

1. Preheat the oven to 200°C/400°F/Gas Mark 6. Place 12 paper cases in a muffin tin. Sift together the flour and baking powder into a small bowl. Stir in the sugar. Add the peanut butter and stir until the mixture resembles breadcrumbs. Transfer the mixture to a large bowl.

2. Lightly beat the egg in a large jug, then beat in the milk and melted butter. Make a well in the centre of the dry ingredients, pour in the beaten liquid ingredients and add the fudge pieces. Stir gently until just combined; do not over-mix.

3. Divide the mixture evenly between the paper cases. Sprinkle the peanuts over the tops of the muffins. Bake in the preheated oven for 20–25 minutes, or until well risen, golden brown and firm to the touch.

4. Leave the muffins in the tin for 5 minutes, then serve warm or transfer to a wire rack and leave to cool.

2

2

4

Apple Streusel Cupcakes

 MAKES 14   PREP TIME: 25 minutes   COOKING TIME: 20 minutes

nutritional information per cupcake	160 kcals, 6g fat, 3.5g sat fat, 13g total sugars, 0.3g salt

Topped with a spiced crumble, these fruity cupcakes make a great pudding served warm with whipped cream.

INGREDIENTS

½ tsp bicarbonate of soda

280 g/10 oz apple sauce (from a jar)

55 g/2 oz butter, softened, or soft margarine

85 g/3 oz demerara sugar

1 large egg, beaten

175 g/6 oz self-raising flour

½ tsp ground cinnamon

½ tsp freshly grated nutmeg

topping

50 g/1¾ oz plain flour

50 g/1¾ oz demerara sugar

¼ tsp ground cinnamon

¼ tsp freshly grated nutmeg

35 g/1¼ oz butter, softened

1. Preheat the oven to 180°C/350°F/Gas Mark 4. Place 14 paper cases in a bun tin.

2. To make the topping, put the flour, demerara sugar, cinnamon and nutmeg in a bowl. Cut the butter into small pieces, then add to the bowl and rub it in with your fingertips until the mixture resembles fine breadcrumbs.

3. Add the bicarbonate of soda to the apple sauce and stir until dissolved. Place the butter and demerara sugar in a large bowl and beat together until pale and creamy. Gradually beat in the egg. Sift in the flour, cinnamon and nutmeg and, using a metal spoon, fold into the mixture, alternating with the apple sauce mixture.

4. Divide the mixture evenly between the paper cases. Scatter the topping over the cupcakes and press down gently. Bake in the preheated oven for 20 minutes, or until risen, golden and firm to the touch. Transfer to a wire rack and leave to cool.

2

3

3

FREEZING TIP
Freeze for up to two
months packed into a
freezer box. Thaw at
room temperature for
2-3 hours.

Cookies & Bars

Chocolate Chip Cookies

 MAKES 8

 PREP TIME:
10 minutes

 COOKING TIME:
10–12 minutes

nutritional information per biscuit	353 kcals, 19g fat, 6g sat fat, 27g total sugars, 0.5g salt

These American-style, chocolate-laden cookies are crisp on the outside and chewy in the middle. Delicious warm from the oven, they also keep well stored in an airtight container.

INGREDIENTS

unsalted butter, melted, for greasing
175 g/6 oz plain flour, sifted
1 tsp baking powder
125 g/4½ oz margarine, melted
85 g/3 oz light muscovado sugar
55 g/2 oz caster sugar
½ tsp vanilla extract
1 egg, beaten
125 g/4½ oz plain chocolate chips

1. Preheat the oven to 190°C/375°F/Gas Mark 5. Lightly grease two baking sheets.

2. Place all of the ingredients in a large mixing bowl and beat until well combined.

3. Place tablespoons of the mixture on the prepared baking sheets, spaced well apart.

4. Bake in the preheated oven for 10–12 minutes, or until golden brown. Transfer to a wire rack and leave to cool.

1

2

3

SOMETHING DIFFERENT
Add some roughly
chopped nuts to the
cookie mixture - try
pecan nuts, hazelnuts
or blanched almonds.

Double Chocolate Pecan Blondies

 MAKES 12

 PREP TIME:
30 minutes
plus cooling

 COOKING TIME:
35–40 minutes

nutritional information per cake	346 kcals, 21g fat, 9g sat fat, 28g total sugars, 0.25g salt

With chunks of white and dark chocolate and crunchy pecan nuts, these moreish bars are an indulgent treat.

INGREDIENTS

250 g/9 oz white chocolate, broken into pieces

40 g/1½ oz butter, plus extra for greasing

175 g/6 oz plain chocolate

2 large eggs, beaten

85 g/3 oz caster sugar

115 g/4 oz self-raising flour

100 g/3½ oz pecan nuts, roughly chopped

1. Preheat the oven to 180°C/350°F/Gas Mark 4. Grease a 20-cm/ 8-inch shallow square baking tin or baking dish.

2. Place 85 g/3 oz of the white chocolate in a heatproof bowl and add the butter. Set the bowl over a saucepan of gently simmering water and heat, stirring occasionally, until melted and smooth. Meanwhile, roughly chop the remaining white and plain chocolate.

3. Beat the eggs and sugar together in a large bowl then stir in the melted chocolate mixture. Sift the flour over the top. Add the chopped chocolate and pecan nuts. Mix well.

4. Spoon the mixture into the prepared tin and smooth the surface. Bake in the preheated oven for 35–40 minutes, or until golden brown and just firm to the touch in the centre. Leave in the tin until completely cooled and the chocolate chunks inside have set, then turn out and cut into pieces.

2

3

4

COOK'S NOTE
Take care not
to over cook the
blondies or you'll
lose that lovely
soft, squidgy
texture.

Vanilla Macaroons

 MAKES 16   PREP TIME: 20 minutes plus cooling    COOKING TIME: 10–15 minutes

nutritional information per cake	125 kcals, 5.5g fat, 2g sat fat, 17.5g total sugars, trace salt

Originating from France, these melt-in-the-mouth petits fours are made with ground almonds, sugar and egg whites.

INGREDIENTS

75 g/2¾ oz ground almonds
115 g/4 oz icing sugar
2 large egg whites
50 g/1¾ oz caster sugar
½ tsp vanilla extract

filling
55 g/2 oz unsalted butter, softened
½ tsp vanilla extract
115 g/4 oz icing sugar, sifted

1. Place the ground almonds and icing sugar in a food processor and process for 15 seconds. Sift the mixture into a bowl. Line two baking sheets with baking paper.

2. Place the egg whites in a clean, grease-free bowl and whisk until holding soft peaks. Gradually whisk in the caster sugar to make a firm, glossy meringue. Whisk in the vanilla extract.

3. Using a spatula, fold the almond mixture into the meringue one third at a time. When all the dry ingredients are thoroughly incorporated, continue to cut and fold the mixture until it forms a shiny batter with a thick, ribbon-like consistency.

4. Pour the mixture into a piping bag fitted with a 1-cm/½-inch plain nozzle. Pipe 32 small rounds onto the prepared baking sheets. Tap the baking sheets firmly onto a work surface to remove air bubbles. Leave at room temperature for 30 minutes. Preheat the oven to 160°C/325°F/Gas Mark 3.

5. Bake in the preheated oven for 10–15 minutes. Cool for 10 minutes, then carefully peel the macaroons off the baking paper. Leave to cool completely.

6. To make the filling, beat the butter and vanilla extract in a bowl until pale and fluffy. Gradually beat in the icing sugar until smooth and creamy. Use to sandwich pairs of macaroons together.

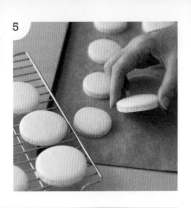

Cinnamon Stars

 MAKES 20

 PREP TIME:
25 minutes
plus chilling

 COOKING TIME:
25 minutes

nutritional information per biscuit	116 kcals, 8g fat, 0.6g sat fat, 9g total sugars, trace salt

These beautiful little spiced hazelnut star cookies are perfect to give as a home-made Christmas gift.

INGREDIENTS

2 egg whites

175 g/6 oz icing sugar, plus extra for dusting

250 g/9 oz ground hazelnuts, roasted

1 tbsp ground cinnamon

1. Whisk the egg whites in a clean, grease-free bowl until stiff. Stir in the sugar until thoroughly combined and then continue to whisk until thick and glossy.

2. Remove 40 g/1½ oz of this mixture and set aside. Then fold the hazelnuts and cinnamon into the remaining mixture to make a very stiff dough. Chill in the refrigerator for about an hour.

3. Preheat the oven to 140°C/275°F/Gas Mark 1. Line two baking sheets with baking paper. Roll out the dough to 1 cm/½ inch thick on a surface amply floured with icing sugar.

4. Cut the dough into shapes using a 5-cm/2-inch star-shaped cutter, dusting with icing sugar to prevent sticking. Re-roll as necessary until all of the mixture is used up.

5. Place the cookies on the prepared baking sheets, spaced well apart, and spread the top of each star with the reserved egg white icing.

6. Bake in the preheated oven for 25 minutes, or until the cookies are still white and crisp on top but slightly soft and moist underneath. Turn off the oven and open the oven door to release the heat and dry the cookies out in the oven for 10 more minutes. Transfer to wire racks to cool completely.

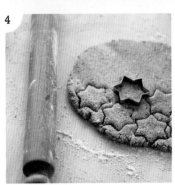

Raisin Flapjacks

nutritional information per slice	147 kcals, 8g fat, 5g sat fat, 12g total sugars, 0.15g salt

These simple flapjacks have a sweet buttery flavour and are studded with juicy raisins. You can replace the raisins with sultanas or currants or try milk or plain chocolate chips instead.

INGREDIENTS

140 g/5 oz rolled oats

115 g/4 oz demerara sugar

85 g/3 oz raisins

115 g/4 oz butter, melted, plus extra for greasing

1. Preheat the oven to 190°C/375°F/Gas Mark 5. Grease a 28 x 18-cm/11 x 7-inch shallow baking tin.

2. Combine the oats, sugar and raisins with the butter in a mixing bowl, stirring well. Spoon the mixture into the prepared tin and press down firmly with the back of a spoon. Bake in the preheated oven for 15–20 minutes, or until golden.

3. Using a sharp knife, mark into 14 bars, then leave to cool in the tin for 10 minutes. Carefully transfer the bars to a wire rack to cool completely.

2

2

3

HEALTHY HINT
Cut the flapjacks into smaller pieces for a less calorific sweet treat.

Sugar Cookies

 MAKES 20   PREP TIME: 20 minutes plus chilling   COOKING TIME 10–12 minutes

nutritional information per biscuit	90 kcals, 5g fat, 3g sat fat, 3g total sugars, trace salt

Crisp, light and buttery with a hint of lemon and a sweet sugary coating - the perfect cookie!

INGREDIENTS

115 g/4 oz butter, softened, plus extra for greasing

55 g/2 oz caster sugar, plus extra for sprinkling

1 tsp finely grated lemon rind

1 egg yolk

175 g/6 oz plain flour, plus extra for dusting

1. Place the butter and sugar in a bowl and beat together until pale and creamy. Beat in the lemon rind and egg yolk. Sift in the flour and mix to a soft dough. Turn out onto a floured work surface and knead until smooth, adding a little more flour, if necessary. Halve the dough, shape into balls, wrap in clingfilm and chill in the refrigerator for 1 hour.

2. Preheat the oven to 180°C/350°F/Gas Mark 4. Lightly grease two large baking sheets.

3. Roll out the dough on a lightly floured work surface to a thickness of 5 mm/¼ inch. Using 7-cm/2¾-inch flower-shaped and heart-shaped cutters stamp out 20 cookies, re-rolling the dough as necessary. Place on the prepared baking sheets and sprinkle with sugar.

4. Bake in the preheated oven for 10–12 minutes, or until pale golden. Leave to cool on the baking sheets for 2–3 minutes, then transfer to a wire rack to cool completely.

1
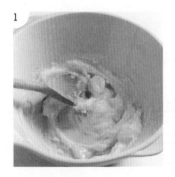

3

3
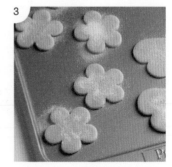

Double Chocolate Whoopie Pies

 MAKES 12

 PREP TIME:
30 minutes
plus chilling

 COOKING TIME:
20–25 minutes

nutritional information per cake	480 kcals, 35g fat, 19g sat fat, 26g total sugars, 0.8g salt

An American invention, whoopie pies are soft rounds of sponge with a delicious creamy filling. This double chocolate version is simply irresistible.

INGREDIENTS

200 g/7 oz plain flour
1½ tsp bicarbonate of soda
25 g/1 oz cocoa powder
large pinch of salt
85 g/3 oz butter, softened
85 g/3 oz white vegetable fat
150 g/5½ oz soft light brown sugar
25 g/1 oz plain chocolate, finely grated
1 large egg, beaten
125 ml/4 fl oz milk
4 tbsp plain chocolate strands

white chocolate filling
175 g/6 oz white chocolate, broken into pieces
2 tbsp milk
300 ml/10 fl oz double cream

1. Preheat the oven to 180°C/350°F/Gas Mark 4. Line two to three baking sheets with baking paper. Sift together the plain flour, bicarbonate of soda, cocoa powder and salt.

2. Place the butter, white vegetable fat, sugar and grated chocolate in a large bowl and beat with an electric handheld whisk until pale and fluffy. Beat in the egg followed by half the flour mixture then the milk. Stir in the rest of the flour mixture and mix until thoroughly incorporated.

3. Pipe or spoon 24 mounds of the mixture onto the prepared baking sheets, spaced well apart to allow for spreading. Bake in the preheated oven, one sheet at a time, for 10–12 minutes, or until risen and just firm to the touch. Cool for 5 minutes then, using a palette knife, transfer to a wire rack and leave to cool completely.

4. For the filling, place the chocolate and milk in a heatproof bowl set over a saucepan of simmering water. Heat until the chocolate has melted, stirring occasionally. Remove from the heat and leave to cool for 30 minutes. Using an electric whisk, whip the cream until holding firm peaks. Fold in the chocolate. Cover and chill in the refrigerator for 30–45 minutes, or until firm enough to spread.

5. To assemble, spread or pipe the chocolate filling on the flat side of half of the cakes. Top with the rest of the cakes. Spread the chocolate strands on a plate and gently roll the edges of each whoopie pie in the strands to lightly coat.

Classic Oatmeal Cookies

 MAKES 30

 PREP TIME:
15 minutes

 COOKING TIME:
15 minutes

nutritional information
per biscuit | 141 kcals, 6g fat, 3g sat fat, 9g total sugars, 0.3g salt

These simple cookies are made from storecupboard ingredients and take minutes to make and bake.

INGREDIENTS

175 g/6 oz butter, softened,
plus extra for greasing
275 g/9¾ oz demerara sugar
1 egg, beaten
4 tbsp water
1 tsp vanilla extract
375 g/13 oz rolled oats
140 g/5 oz plain flour
1 tsp salt
½ tsp bicarbonate of soda

1. Preheat the oven to 180°C/350°F/Gas Mark 4. Grease two large baking sheets.

2. Place the butter and sugar in a large bowl and beat together until pale and creamy. Beat in the egg, water and vanilla extract until the mixture is smooth. Mix the oats, flour, salt and bicarbonate of soda together in a separate bowl, then gradually stir the oat mixture into the creamed mixture until thoroughly combined.

3. Place tablespoonfuls of the mixture on the prepared baking sheets, spaced well apart.

4. Bake in the preheated oven for 15 minutes, or until golden brown. Transfer to a wire rack to cool completely.

COOK'S NOTE
To get even-sized cookies, use a small ice-cream scoop to measure out the dough.

Butterscotch Cookies

 MAKES 22 PREP TIME 20 minutes COOKING TIME 8–10 minutes

nutritional information per biscuit	118 kcals, 5.5g fat, 3g sat fat, 9.5g total sugars, 0.35g salt

Chunks of melted toffee give these golden brown cookies a deliciously chewy texture.

INGREDIENTS

175 g/6 oz soft light brown sugar
115 g/4 oz butter, softened
1 large egg, beaten
1 tsp vanilla extract
200 g/7 oz self-raising flour
1 tsp bicarbonate of soda
10 dairy toffees, chopped

1. Preheat the oven to 180°C/350°F/Gas Mark 4. Line three large baking sheets with baking paper.

2. Put the sugar and butter into a bowl and beat together until creamy. Beat in the egg and vanilla extract. Sift together the flour and bicarbonate of soda and stir in thoroughly. Stir in the toffees.

3. Place walnut-sized spoonfuls of the mixture on the prepared baking sheets, spaced well apart.

4. Bake in the preheated oven for 8–10 minutes, or until light golden brown. Leave to cool on the baking sheets, then peel away from the baking paper.

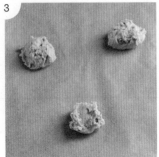

COOK'S NOTE
Leave the toffees in a warm place for about 30 minutes before chopping to allow them to soften a little.

Chocolate & Cinnamon Brownies

 MAKES 16   PREP TIME: 40 minutes plus cooling   COOKING TIME: 35–40 minutes

nutritional information per cake	348 kcals, 19g fat, 9g sat fat, 29g total sugars, 0.3g salt

An American favourite, chocolate brownies are really easy to make, keep well and always taste fantastic. This version is full of pecan nuts, lightly spiced with ground cinnamon and topped with a sweet white chocolate frosting.

INGREDIENTS

115 g/4 oz plain chocolate, broken into pieces
175 g/6 oz butter, plus extra for greasing
85 g/3 oz pecan nut halves
250 g/9 oz caster sugar
4 eggs, beaten
225 g/8 oz plain flour
2 tsp ground cinnamon

frosting
25 g/1 oz butter
55 g/2 oz white chocolate, broken into pieces
2 tbsp milk
115 g/4 oz icing sugar

1. Preheat the oven to 180°C/350°F/Gas Mark 4. Grease a 23-cm/9-inch shallow square cake tin.

2. Melt the plain chocolate and butter in a heatproof bowl, set over a saucepan of gently simmering water. Remove from the heat and allow to cool slightly.

3. Set 16 pecan halves to one side for decoration and chop the rest. Beat together the caster sugar and eggs with a whisk until thick and creamy. Then fold in the chocolate mixture, flour, cinnamon and chopped pecans.

4. Transfer the mixture to the prepared tin and bake in the preheated oven for 35–40 minutes, or until just firm to the touch. Leave to cool in the tin.

5. To make the frosting, melt the butter and white chocolate in a heatproof bowl, set over a saucepan of gently simmering water. Remove from the heat and beat in the milk and icing sugar. Spread this mixture over the cooled brownies. Allow to set for 30 minutes then cut into 16 squares and top each square with a pecan half.

Peanut Butter Cookies

 MAKES 15

 PREP TIME:
20 minutes
plus chilling

 COOKING TIME:
15 minutes

nutritional information
per biscuit   260 kcals, 15g fat, 6g sat fat, 16g total sugars, 0.5g salt

Rich and buttery with a lovely peanut flavour, these simple cookies taste great with a glass of cold milk.

INGREDIENTS

175 g/6 oz plain flour
½ tsp baking powder
½ tsp salt
225 g/8 oz smooth peanut butter
115 g/4 oz butter, softened
1¼ tsp vanilla extract
115 g/4 oz brown sugar
100 g/3½ oz caster sugar
2 eggs

1. Sift together the flour, baking powder and salt into a bowl and set aside. Beat together the peanut butter, butter and vanilla extract until smooth in another bowl. Beat in the brown and caster sugars for 1 minute, then beat in the eggs one at a time. Stir in the flour mixture in two batches.

2. Halve the dough, shape into balls, wrap in clingfilm and chill in the refrigerator for at least 2 hours. Meanwhile, preheat the oven to 180°C/350°F/Gas Mark 4. Line two baking sheets with baking paper or leave uncovered and ungreased.

3. Roll or scoop the dough into 4-cm/1½-inch balls and place them on the prepared baking sheets, spaced well apart. Use a fork to flatten each ball by making a criss-cross pattern. Bake in the preheated oven for 15 minutes, or until golden. Remove the biscuits from the oven and leave to cool on the baking sheet for 5 minutes. Using a palette knife, transfer to a wire rack to cool completely.

1

2

3

BE PREPARED
The wrapped cookie dough can be kept in the refrigerator for 2-3 days before baking.

Apricot Flapjacks

 MAKES 10   PREP TIME: 15 minutes   COOKING TIME: 20–25 minutes

nutritional information per slice	296 kcals, 17g fat, 3.5g sat fat, 18g total sugars, 0.3g salt

Flapjacks are really easy to make and taste so much better than shop-bought. Great for packed lunches or fibre-packed snacks, this version is flavoured with apricots, honey and sesame seeds.

INGREDIENTS

175 g/6 oz margarine, plus extra for greasing

85 g/3 oz demerara sugar

55 g/2 oz clear honey

140 g/5 oz dried apricots, chopped

2 tsp sesame seeds

225 g/8 oz rolled oats

1. Preheat the oven to 180°C/350°F/Gas Mark 4. Grease a 26 x 17-cm/10½ x 6½-inch shallow baking tin.

2. Put the margarine, sugar and honey into a small saucepan over a low heat and heat until the ingredients have melted together – do not boil. When the ingredients are well combined, stir in the apricots, sesame seeds and oats.

3. Spoon the mixture into the prepared tin and smooth the surface with the back of a spoon. Bake in the preheated oven for 20–25 minutes, or until golden brown.

4. Remove from the oven, cut into 10 bars and leave to cool completely before removing from the tin.

COOK'S NOTE
Flapjacks are still soft when they come straight out of the oven – they set on cooling.

Salted Caramel Squares

 MAKES 16

 PREP TIME
30 minutes
plus chilling

 COOKING TIME
15 minutes

nutritional information per slice	356 kcals, 21g fat, 12g sat fat, 29g total sugars, 0.5g salt

A touch of sea salt added to the caramel gives this sweet treat a modern twist.

INGREDIENTS

115 g/4 oz butter, softened, plus extra for greasing
55 g/2 oz caster sugar
175 g/6 oz plain flour
55 g/2 oz ground almonds

topping
175 g/6 oz butter
115 g/4 oz caster sugar
3 tbsp golden syrup
400 ml/14 fl oz canned condensed milk
¼ tsp sea salt crystals
85 g/3 oz plain chocolate, melted

1. Preheat the oven to 180°C/350°F/Gas Mark 4. Grease a 20-cm/8-inch shallow square cake tin.

2. Put the butter and sugar into a bowl and beat together until pale and creamy. Sift in the flour and add the ground almonds. Use clean hands to mix and knead to a crumbly dough. Press into the base of the prepared tin and prick the surface all over with a fork. Bake in the preheated oven for 15 minutes, or until pale golden. Leave to cool.

3. To make the topping, put the butter, sugar, golden syrup and condensed milk into a saucepan over a low heat and heat gently until the sugar has dissolved. Increase the heat to medium, bring to the boil, then simmer for 6–8 minutes, stirring constantly, until the mixture becomes very thick. Stir in half the salt, then quickly pour the caramel over the shortbread base. Sprinkle over the remaining salt.

4. Spoon the chocolate into a paper piping bag and snip off the end. Pipe the chocolate over the caramel and swirl with the tip of a knife. Leave to cool, then chill for 2 hours, or until firm. Cut into 16 squares.

2

3

4

COOK'S NOTE

A heavy-based saucepan is essential for making the caramel and you must stir the mixture constantly to prevent burning.

Marshmallow S'mores

 MAKES 15

 PREP TIME:
30 minutes
plus chilling

 COOKING TIME
12–17 minutes

nutritional information per biscuit	371 kcals, 20g fat, 12g sat fat, 30g total sugars, 0.4g salt

The name s'mores is a shortened version of 'some more' – and everyone will want more of these chocolate cookies with a marshmallow filling!

INGREDIENTS

225 g/8 oz butter, softened
140 g/5 oz caster sugar
2 tsp finely grated orange rind
1 egg yolk, lightly beaten
250 g/9 oz plain flour
25 g/1 oz cocoa powder
½ tsp ground cinnamon
pinch of salt
30 yellow marshmallows, halved horizontally
300 g/10½ oz plain chocolate, broken into pieces
4 tbsp orange marmalade
15 walnut halves, to decorate

1. Place the butter, sugar and orange rind in a large bowl and beat together until light and fluffy, then beat in the egg yolk. Sift together the flour, cocoa, cinnamon and salt into the mixture and stir until combined. Halve the dough, shape into balls, wrap in clingfilm and chill in the refrigerator for 30–60 minutes.

2. Preheat the oven to 190°C/375°F/Gas Mark 5. Line several large baking sheets with baking paper. Unwrap the dough and roll out between two sheets of baking paper. Cut out 30 cookies with a 6-cm/2½-inch fluted round cutter and place them on the prepared baking sheets, spaced well apart. Bake in the preheated oven for 10–15 minutes. Leave to cool for 5 minutes. Turn half the cookies upside down and put four marshmallow halves on each. Bake these cookies with marshmallows on for a further 1–2 minutes. Leave all the cookies on wire racks for 30 minutes.

3. Place the chocolate in a heatproof bowl, set the bowl over a saucepan of gently simmering water and heat until melted. Line a baking sheet with baking paper. Spread the marmalade over the undersides of the uncovered cookies and place them on top of the marshmallow-covered cookies. Dip the cookies in the melted chocolate to coat. Place a walnut half in the centre of each cookie and leave to set.

Sweet Bakes & Breads

Apple Pie

 SERVES 6

 PREP TIME:
40 minutes
plus chilling

 COOKING TIME:
50 minutes

nutritional information per serving	567 kcals, 28g fat, 13.5g sat fat, 32g total sugars, 0.5g salt

A golden pastry case filled to the brim with apples, sugar and a hint of cinnamon – this is the ultimate apple pie!

INGREDIENTS

pastry
350 g/12 oz plain flour, plus extra for dusting

pinch of salt

85 g/3 oz butter or margarine, diced

85 g/3 oz lard or white vegetable fat, diced

6 tbsp cold water

beaten egg or milk, for glazing

filling
750 g–1 kg/1 lb 10 oz–2 lb 4 oz cooking apples, peeled, cored and sliced

125 g/4½ oz caster sugar, plus extra for sprinkling

½–1 tsp ground cinnamon, mixed spice or ground ginger

1. To make the pastry, sift the flour and salt into a mixing bowl. Add the butter and lard and rub in with your fingertips until the mixture resembles fine breadcrumbs. Add the water and gather the mixture together into a dough. Wrap the dough in clingfilm and chill in the refrigerator for 30 minutes.

2. Preheat the oven to 220°C/425°F/Gas Mark 7. Roll out almost two thirds of the pastry thinly on a lightly floured surface and use to line a deep 23-cm/9-inch pie dish.

3. To make the filling, place the apple slices, sugar and spice in a bowl and mix together thoroughly. Pack the apple mixture into the pastry case; the filling can come up above the rim. Add 1–2 tablespoons of water if needed, particularly if the apples are not very juicy.

4. Roll out the remaining pastry on a lightly floured surface to form a lid. Dampen the edges of the pie rim with water and position the lid, pressing the edges firmly together. Trim and crimp the edges. Use the trimmings to cut out leaves or other shapes to decorate the top of the pie. Dampen and attach. Glaze the top of the pie with beaten egg, make 1–2 slits in the top and place the pie dish on a baking sheet.

5. Bake in the preheated oven for 20 minutes, then reduce the temperature to 180°C/350°F/Gas Mark 4 and bake for a further 30 minutes, or until the pastry is a light golden brown. Serve hot or cold, sprinkled with sugar.

Five-Grain Loaf

 MAKES
1 loaf

 PREP TIME:
20 minutes
plus rising

 COOKING TIME:
25–30 minutes

nutritional information per loaf	2544 kcals, 84g fat, 12g sat fat, 24g total sugars, 4.8g salt

Packed full of nutritious seeds and made with wholemeal flour, this loaf is full of fibre.

INGREDIENTS

300 g/10½ oz strong wholemeal flour, plus extra for dusting

225 g/8 oz strong white flour

1 tsp salt

100 g/3½ oz five-seed mix (including sesame, pumpkin, sunflower, hemp and linseeds)

7 g/¼ oz easy-blend dried yeast

1 tbsp soft light brown sugar

2 tbsp sunflower oil, plus extra for greasing

300 ml/10 fl oz lukewarm water

1. Lightly grease a baking sheet with oil. Mix the wholemeal flour, white flour, salt, seed mix and yeast in a large bowl. Stir in the sugar. Mix together the oil and water. Make a well in the centre and pour in the liquid. Mix with a knife to make a soft sticky dough.

2. Turn out the dough onto a lightly floured work surface and knead for 5–7 minutes, or until smooth and elastic. Shape the dough into a round ball and place on the prepared baking sheet. Dust the top of the loaf with wholemeal flour and leave in a warm place for 1–1½ hours, or until doubled in size.

3. Meanwhile, preheat the oven to 220°C/425°F/Gas Mark 7. Bake in the preheated oven for 5 minutes. Reduce the oven temperature to 200°C/400°F/Gas Mark 6 and bake for a further 20–25 minutes, or until golden brown and the base sounds hollow when tapped with your knuckles. Transfer to a wire rack to cool.

1

2

3

SOMETHING
DIFFERENT
To make individual
rolls, divide and
shape the dough into
12 round balls and
bake for 10-15
minutes at
200°C/400°F/
Gas Mark 6.

Key Lime Pie

 SERVES 8

 PREP TIME:
30 minutes
plus chilling

 COOKING TIME:
20 minutes

nutritional information
per serving 377 kcals, 19g fat, 10g sat fat, 33g total sugars, 0.7g salt

This refreshing sweet lime pie originates from the Florida Keys in America and is named after the limes that are grown in the area.

INGREDIENTS

crumb crust
175 g/6 oz digestive or ginger biscuits
2 tbsp caster sugar
½ tsp ground cinnamon
70 g/2½ oz butter, melted, plus extra for greasing

filling
400 ml/14 fl oz canned condensed milk
125 ml/4 fl oz freshly squeezed lime juice
finely grated rind of 3 limes
4 egg yolks
whipped cream, to serve

1. Preheat the oven to 160°C/325°F/Gas Mark 3. Lightly grease a 23-cm/9-inch tart tin, about 4 cm/1½ inches deep. To make the crumb crust, put the biscuits, sugar and cinnamon in a food processor and process until fine crumbs form – do not overprocess to a powder. Add the melted butter and process again until moistened.

2. Tip the crumb mixture into the prepared tart tin and press over the base and up the sides. Place the tart tin on a baking sheet and bake in the preheated oven for 5 minutes. Meanwhile, to make the filling, beat the condensed milk, lime juice, lime rind and egg yolks together in a bowl until well blended.

3. Remove the tart tin from the oven, pour the filling into the crumb crust and spread out to the edges. Return to the oven for a further 15 minutes, or until the filling is set around the edges but still wobbly in the centre. Leave to cool completely on a wire rack, then cover and chill for at least 2 hours. Spread with whipped cream and serve.

1

2

3

SOMETHING
DIFFERENT
Instead of
cream, top the
pie with meringue
and brown briefly
in a hot oven.

Wholemeal Loaf

 MAKES
1 loaf

 PREP TIME
20 minutes
plus rising

 COOKING TIME
30 minutes

nutritional information per loaf	1024 kcals, 27g fat, 3g sat fat, 34g total sugars, 5g salt

Made with wholemeal flour which contains the whole wheat grain, this loaf will have more flavour, fibre and nutrients than white bread.

INGREDIENTS

225 g/8 oz strong wholemeal flour, plus extra for dusting

1 tbsp skimmed milk powder

1 tsp salt

2 tbsp soft light brown sugar

1 tsp easy-blend dried yeast

1½ tbsp sunflower oil, plus extra for greasing

175 ml/6 fl oz lukewarm water

1. Place the flour, milk powder, salt, sugar and yeast in a large bowl. Pour in the oil and add the water, then mix well to make a smooth dough.

2. Turn out onto a lightly floured surface and knead well for about 10 minutes, or until smooth. Brush a bowl with oil. Shape the dough into a ball, place it in the bowl and cover with a damp tea towel. Leave to rise in a warm place for 1 hour, or until the dough has doubled in volume.

3. Preheat the oven to 220°C/425°F/Gas Mark 7. Oil a 900-g/2-lb loaf tin. Turn the dough out onto a lightly floured surface and knead for 1 minute, or until smooth. Shape the dough the length of the tin and three times the width. Fold the dough into three lengthways and place it in the tin with the join underneath. Cover and leave in a warm place for 30 minutes, or until it has risen above the tin.

4. Place in the preheated oven and bake for 30 minutes, or until firm and golden brown. Test that the loaf is cooked by tapping on the base with your knuckles – it should sound hollow. Transfer to a wire rack to cool.

Pumpkin Pie

 SERVES 8

 PREP TIME:
25 minutes

 COOKING TIME:
1 hour

nutritional information per serving	630 kcals, 42g fat, 21g sat fat, 33g total sugars, 0.98g salt

This traditional American pie makes a lovely autumnal dessert and it's a great way to use up pumpkin flesh carved from Hallowe'en lanterns.

INGREDIENTS

plain flour, for dusting
350 g/12 oz ready-made shortcrust pastry
400 g/14 oz pumpkin purée
2 eggs, lightly beaten
150 g/5½ oz sugar
1 tsp ground cinnamon
½ tsp ground ginger
¼ tsp ground cloves
½ tsp salt
350 ml/12 fl oz canned evaporated milk

eggnog whipped cream
350 ml/12 fl oz double cream
70 g/2½ oz icing sugar
1 tbsp brandy, or to taste
1 tbsp light or dark rum, or to taste
freshly grated nutmeg, to decorate

1. Preheat the oven to 200°C/400°F/Gas Mark 6. Very lightly dust a rolling pin with flour and use to roll out the pastry on a lightly floured work surface into a 30-cm/12-inch round. Line a 23-cm/9-inch deep pie dish with the pastry, trimming the excess. Line the pastry case with baking paper and fill with dried beans.

2. Bake blind in the preheated oven for 10 minutes. Remove from the oven and take out the paper and beans. Reduce the oven temperature to 180°C/350°F/Gas Mark 4.

3. Meanwhile, put the pumpkin purée, eggs, sugar, cinnamon, ginger, cloves and salt into a bowl and beat together, then beat in the evaporated milk. Pour the mixture into the pastry case, return to the oven, and bake for 40–50 minutes until the filling is set and a knife inserted in the centre comes out clean. Transfer to a wire rack and set aside to cool completely.

4. While the pie is baking, make the eggnog whipped cream. Put the cream in a bowl and beat until it has thickened and increased in volume. Just as it starts to stiffen, sift over the icing sugar and continue beating until it holds stiff peaks. Add the brandy and rum and beat, taking care not to overbeat or the mixture will separate. Cover and chill until required. When ready to serve, grate some nutmeg over the whipped cream. Serve the pie with the cream.

Lemon Meringue Pie

 SERVES 8

 PREP TIME:
40 minutes
plus chilling

 COOKING TIME:
55 minutes

nutritional information per serving	300 kcals, 12g fat, 6.5g sat fat, 27g total sugars, 0.25g salt

The beauty of this classic English dessert is the way the sweet pastry case and sugary meringue perfectly complement the deliciously tangy lemon filling.

INGREDIENTS

pastry
150 g/5½ oz plain flour, plus extra for dusting
85 g/3 oz butter, diced, plus extra for greasing
35 g/1¼ oz icing sugar, sifted
finely grated rind of ½ lemon
½ egg yolk, beaten
1½ tbsp milk

filling
3 tbsp cornflour
300 ml/10 fl oz water
juice and grated rind of 2 lemons
175 g/6 oz caster sugar
2 eggs, separated

1. To make the pastry, sift the flour into a bowl. Rub in the butter with your fingertips until the mixture resembles fine breadcrumbs. Mix in the remaining pastry ingredients. Turn out onto a lightly floured work surface and knead briefly. Wrap in clingfilm and chill in the refrigerator for 30 minutes.

2. Preheat the oven to 180°C/350°F/Gas Mark 4. Grease a 20-cm/8-inch tart tin. Roll out the pastry to a thickness of 5 mm/¼ inch on a lightly floured surface, then use it to line the base and sides of the tin. Prick all over with a fork, line with baking paper and fill with baking beans. Bake blind in the preheated oven for 15 minutes. Remove the pastry case from the oven and take out the paper and beans. Reduce the oven temperature to 150°C/300°F/Gas Mark 2.

3. To make the filling, mix the cornflour with a little of the water to form a paste. Put the remaining water in a saucepan. Stir in the lemon juice, lemon rind and cornflour paste. Bring to the boil, stirring. Cook for 2 minutes. Leave to cool slightly. Stir in 5 tablespoons of the caster sugar and the egg yolks, then pour into the pastry case.

4. Whisk the egg whites in a clean, grease-free bowl until they hold stiff peaks. Gradually whisk in the remaining caster sugar and spread over the pie. Bake for a further 40 minutes. Remove from the oven, cool and serve.

Crusty White Loaf

 MAKES
1 loaf

 PREP TIME
20 minutes
plus rising

 COOKING TIME
30 minutes

nutritional information
per loaf | 2123 kcals, 42g fat, 18g sat fat, 17g total sugars, 7.7g salt

Baking your own bread is a satisfying and rewarding pastime. If you're a novice baker then start with this simple white loaf.

INGREDIENTS

1 egg

1 egg yolk

150–200 ml/5–7 fl oz lukewarm water

500 g/1 lb 2 oz strong white flour, plus extra for dusting

1½ tsp salt

2 tsp sugar

1 tsp easy-blend dried yeast

25 g/1 oz butter, diced

sunflower oil, for greasing

1. Place the egg and egg yolk in a jug and beat lightly to mix. Add enough lukewarm water to make up to 300 ml/10 fl oz. Stir well.

2. Place the flour, salt, sugar and yeast in a large bowl. Add the butter and rub it in with your fingertips until the mixture resembles breadcrumbs. Make a well in the centre, add the egg mixture and work to a smooth dough.

3. Turn out onto a lightly floured surface and knead well for about 10 minutes, or until smooth. Brush a bowl with oil. Shape the dough into a ball, place it in the bowl and cover with a damp tea towel. Leave to rise in a warm place for 1 hour, or until the dough has doubled in volume. Preheat the oven to 220°C/425°F/Gas Mark 7. Oil a 900-g/2-lb loaf tin. Turn out the dough onto a lightly floured surface and knead for 1 minute, or until smooth. Shape the dough the length of the tin and three times the width. Fold the dough into three lengthways and place it in the tin with the join underneath. Cover and leave in a warm place for 30 minutes, or until it has risen above the tin.

4. Place in the preheated oven and bake for 30 minutes, or until firm and golden brown. Test that the loaf is cooked by tapping on the base with your knuckles – it should sound hollow. Transfer to a wire rack to cool.

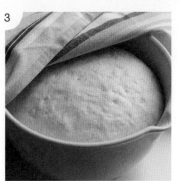

Latticed Cherry Pie

 SERVES 8

 PREP TIME:
40 minutes
plus chilling

 COOKING TIME:
45 minutes

nutritional information per serving	345 kcals, 12.5g fat, 7.5g sat fat, 37g total sugars, 0.4g salt

This colourful pie is full of juicy cherries in a sweet almond - and cherry brandy-flavoured syrup.

INGREDIENTS

pastry

140 g/5 oz plain flour, plus extra for dusting

¼ tsp baking powder

½ tsp mixed spice

½ tsp salt

50 g/1¾ oz caster sugar

55 g/2 oz unsalted butter, chilled and diced, plus extra for greasing

1 egg, beaten, plus extra for glazing

filling

900 g/2 lb stoned fresh cherries, or canned cherries, drained

150 g/5½ oz caster sugar

½ tsp almond extract

2 tsp cherry brandy

¼ tsp mixed spice

2 tbsp cornflour

2 tbsp water

25 g/1 oz unsalted butter, melted

ice cream, to serve

1. To make the pastry, sift the flour with the baking powder into a large bowl. Stir in the mixed spice, salt and sugar. Rub in the butter until the mixture resembles fine breadcrumbs, make a well in the centre, pour in the egg and mix into a dough. Cut the dough in half, and use your hands to roll each half into a ball. Wrap in clingfilm and chill in the refrigerator for 30 minutes.

2. Preheat the oven to 220°C/425°F/Gas Mark 7. Grease a 23-cm/9-inch pie dish. Roll out the doughs into two rounds, each 30 cm/12 inches in diameter. Use one to line the pie dish.

3. To make the filling, put half the cherries and all the sugar in a saucepan. Bring to a simmer and stir in the almond extract, brandy and mixed spice. In a bowl, mix the cornflour and water into a paste. Stir the paste into the saucepan, then boil until the mixture thickens. Stir in the remaining cherries, pour into the pastry case, then dot with the melted butter. Cut the remaining pastry into strips 1 cm/½ inch wide. Lay the strips over the filling, crossing to form a lattice. Trim and seal the edges with water. Use your fingers to crimp around the rim, then glaze the top with the beaten egg.

4. Cover the pie with foil, then bake for 30 minutes in the preheated oven. Remove from the oven, discard the foil, then bake for a further 15 minutes, or until golden. Serve with ice cream.

Sourdough Bread

 MAKES
2 loaves

 PREP TIME:
30 minutes plus
starter and rising

 COOKING TIME:
30 minutes

nutritional information per loaf	1302 kcals, 23g fat, 5g sat fat, 49g total sugars, 10.3g salt

You'll need to plan ahead to make this rustic bread by preparing the starter dough a few days in advance.

INGREDIENTS

450 g/1 lb wholemeal flour
4 tsp salt
350 ml/12 fl oz lukewarm water
2 tbsp black treacle
1 tbsp vegetable oil, plus extra for brushing
plain flour, for dusting

starter
85 g/3 oz wholemeal flour
85 g/3 oz strong white flour
55 g/2 oz caster sugar
250 ml/9 fl oz milk

1. For the starter, put the wholemeal flour, strong white flour, sugar and milk into a non-metallic bowl and beat well with a fork. Cover with a damp tea towel and leave to stand at room temperature for 4–5 days, until the mixture is frothy and smells sour.

2. Sift the flour and half the salt together into a bowl and add the water, treacle, oil and starter. Mix well with a wooden spoon until a dough begins to form, then knead with your hands until it leaves the side of the bowl. Turn out onto a lightly floured surface and knead for 10 minutes, or until smooth and elastic.

3. Brush a bowl with oil. Form the dough into a ball, put it into the bowl and put the bowl into a polythene bag or cover with a damp tea towel. Leave to rise in a warm place for 2 hours, or until the dough has doubled in volume.

4. Dust two baking sheets with flour. Mix the remaining salt with 4 tablespoons of water in a bowl. Turn out the dough onto a lightly floured work surface and knock back with your fist, then knead for a further 10 minutes. Halve the dough, shape each piece into an oval and place the loaves on the prepared baking sheets. Brush with the saltwater glaze and leave to stand in a warm place, brushing frequently with the glaze, for 30 minutes.

5. Preheat the oven to 220°C/425°F/Gas Mark 7. Brush the loaves with the remaining glaze and dust with flour. Bake for 30 minutes, or until the crust is golden brown and the loaves sound hollow when tapped on their bases with your knuckles. If it is necessary to cook them for longer, reduce the oven temperature to 190°C/375°F/Gas Mark 5. Transfer to wire racks to cool.

Cinnamon Swirls

 MAKES 12   PREP TIME: 1 hour   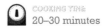 COOKING TIME: 20–30 minutes

nutritional information
per pastry | 170 kcals, 8g fat, 5g sat fat, 9g total sugars, 0.3g salt

These home-made Danish pastries taste delicious warm from the oven for a mid-morning treat.

INGREDIENTS

225 g/8 oz strong white flour
½ tsp salt
7 g/¼ oz easy-blend dried yeast
2 tbsp butter, cut into small pieces, plus extra for greasing
1 egg, lightly beaten
125 ml/4 fl oz lukewarm milk
2 tbsp maple syrup, for glazing

filling
4 tbsp butter, softened
2 tsp ground cinnamon
50 g/1¾ oz soft light brown sugar
50 g/1¾ oz currants

1. Grease a baking sheet with a little butter.

2. Sift the flour and salt into a mixing bowl. Stir in the yeast. Rub in the butter with your fingertips until the mixture resembles breadcrumbs. Add the egg and milk and mix to form a dough.

3. Form the dough into a ball, place in a greased bowl, cover with clingfilm and leave to stand in a warm place for about 40 minutes, or until doubled in size. Lightly knock back the dough for 1 minute, then roll out to a rectangle measuring 30 x 23 cm/12 x 9 inches.

4. To make the filling, cream together the butter, cinnamon and sugar until light and fluffy. Spread the filling evenly over the dough rectangle, leaving a 2.5-cm/1-inch border all around. Sprinkle the currants evenly over the top.

5. Roll up the dough from one of the long edges, and press down to seal. Cut the roll into 12 slices. Place them, cut-side down, on the baking sheet, cover and leave to stand for 30 minutes.

6. Meanwhile, preheat the oven to 190°C/375°F/Gas Mark 5. Bake the buns in the preheated oven for 20–30 minutes, or until well risen. Brush with the maple syrup and leave to cool slightly before serving.

Bread Rolls

 MAKES 12

 PREP TIME:
30 minutes
plus rising

 COOKING TIME:
12–15 minutes

nutritional information per roll	173 kcals, 7g fat, 4g sat fat, 2g total sugars, 0.3g salt

These crusty golden bread rolls are particularly good served warm with a steaming bowl of soup.

INGREDIENTS

125 ml/4 fl oz milk

4 tbsp water

5 tbsp butter, softened, plus extra for brushing

350 g/12 oz strong white flour, plus extra for dusting

2¼ tsp easy-blend dried yeast

1 tbsp sugar

½ tsp salt

1 extra large egg, beaten

sunflower oil, for greasing

1. Put the milk, water and 2 tablespoons of the butter into a small saucepan and heat to 43–45°C/110–113°F. Put the flour, yeast, sugar and salt into a large bowl, stir and make a well in the centre. Slowly pour in 6 tablespoons of the milk mixture, then add the egg and beat, drawing in the flour from the side. Add the remaining milk, tablespoon by tablespoon, until a soft dough forms.

2. Grease a bowl and set aside. Turn out the dough onto a lightly floured work surface and knead for 8–10 minutes, or until smooth and elastic. Shape the dough into a ball, roll it around in the greased bowl, cover with clingfilm and set aside for 1 hour, or until doubled in size.

3. Turn out the dough onto a lightly floured work surface and knock back. Cover with the upturned bowl and leave to rest for 10 minutes. Meanwhile, preheat the oven to 200°C/400°F/Gas Mark 6 and dust a baking sheet with flour. Melt the remaining butter in a small saucepan over a medium heat.

4. Lightly dust a rolling pin with flour and use to roll out the dough to a thickness of 5 mm/¼ inch. Use a floured 8-cm/3¼-inch round cookie cutter to cut out 12 rounds, rerolling the trimmings if necessary. Brush the middle of a round with butter. Use a floured chopstick or pencil to make an indentation just off centre, then fold along that indentation and pinch the edges together to seal. Place on the prepared baking sheet, cover with a tea towel and leave to rise while you shape the remaining rolls.

5. Lightly brush the tops of the rolls with butter and bake in the preheated oven for 12–15 minutes, or until the rolls are golden brown and the bases sound hollow when tapped. Transfer to a wire rack to cool.

Apple Turnovers

 MAKES 8   PREP TIME: 40 minutes   COOKING TIME: 15–20 minutes

nutritional information per pastry	326 kcals, 24g fat, 14g sat fat, 14g total sugars, 0.3g salt

Quick and easy to make, these sweet pastries are a great way to use up a glut of apples.

INGREDIENTS

250 g/9 oz ready-made puff pastry, thawed, if frozen
flour, for dusting
milk, for glazing

filling
450 g/1 lb cooking apples, peeled, cored and chopped
grated rind of 1 lemon (optional)
pinch of ground cloves (optional)
3 tbsp sugar

orange sugar
1 tbsp sugar, for sprinkling
finely grated rind of 1 orange

orange cream
250 ml/9 fl oz double cream
grated rind of 1 orange and juice of ½ orange
icing sugar, to taste

1. To make the filling, mix together the apples, lemon rind and ground cloves, if using, but do not add the sugar yet as the juice will then seep out of the apples. For the orange sugar, mix together the sugar and orange rind.

2. Preheat the oven to 220°C/425°F/Gas Mark 7. Roll out the pastry on a floured work surface into a 60 x 30-cm/24 x 12-inch rectangle. Cut the pastry in half lengthways, then across into four to make eight 15-cm/6-inch squares.

3. Mix the sugar into the apple filling. Brush each square lightly with milk and place a little of the apple filling in the centre. Fold over one corner diagonally to meet the opposite one, making a triangular turnover, and press the edges together very firmly. Place on a baking sheet. Repeat with the remaining squares. Brush with milk and sprinkle with the orange sugar. Bake in the preheated oven for 15–20 minutes, or until browned. Leave to cool on a wire rack.

4. For the orange cream, whip the cream, orange rind and orange juice together until thick. Add a little icing sugar to taste and whip again until it just holds soft peaks. Serve the turnovers warm with orange cream.

Cornbread

 MAKES
1 loaf

 PREP TIME:
15 minutes

 COOKING TIME:
30–35 minutes

nutritional information per loaf	3247 kcals, 171g fat, 89g sat fat, 19g total sugars, 12.8g salt

Polenta gives this yeast-free bread a lovely golden colour and distinctive flavour.

INGREDIENTS

vegetable oil, for greasing
175 g/6 oz plain flour
1 tsp salt
4 tsp baking powder
1 tsp caster sugar
280 g/10 oz polenta
115 g/4 oz butter, softened
4 eggs
250 ml/9 fl oz milk
3 tbsp double cream

1. Preheat the oven to 200°C/400°F/Gas Mark 6. Brush a 20-cm/8-inch square cake tin with oil.

2. Sift the flour, salt and baking powder together into a bowl. Add the sugar and polenta and stir to mix. Add the butter and cut into the dry ingredients with a knife, then rub it in with your fingertips until the mixture resembles fine breadcrumbs.

3. Lightly beat the eggs in a bowl with the milk and cream, then stir into the polenta mixture until thoroughly combined.

4. Spoon the mixture into the prepared tin and smooth the surface. Bake in the preheated oven for 30–35 minutes, or until a skewer inserted into the centre of the loaf comes out clean. Remove the tin from the oven and leave to cool for 5–10 minutes, then cut into squares and serve warm.

2

3

4

Coconut Cream Pie

 SERVES 6

 PREP TIME:
30 minutes
plus chilling

 COOKING TIME:
16–18 minutes

nutritional information per serving	753 kcals, 62g fat, 37g sat fat, 12g total sugars, 0.6g salt

A simple pie crust filled with a layer of sweet coconut and vanilla custard and topped with whipped cream and lightly toasted coconut.

INGREDIENTS

250 g/9 oz ready-made shortcrust pastry, thawed, if frozen

2 eggs

55 g/2 oz caster sugar

1 tsp vanilla extract

2 tbsp plain flour, plus extra for dusting

2 tbsp cornflour

150 ml/5 fl oz milk

200 ml/7 fl oz coconut milk

25 g/1 oz desiccated coconut

400 ml/14 fl oz double cream

2 tbsp toasted desiccated coconut, to decorate

1. Preheat the oven to 200°C/400°F/Gas Mark 6. Roll the pastry out on a lightly floured surface and use to line a 20–23-cm/8–9-inch pie dish. Trim and crimp the edges. Prick the base with a fork and chill in the refrigerator for 15 minutes.

2. Line the pastry case with baking paper and baking beans. Bake blind in the preheated oven for 10 minutes. Remove the paper and beans and bake for a further 6–8 minutes, or until golden. Leave to cool.

3. For the filling, whisk together the eggs, sugar and vanilla extract in a bowl. Blend the flour and cornflour to a paste with 4 tablespoons of milk, then whisk the paste into the egg mixture. Heat the remaining milk and coconut milk in a saucepan until almost boiling and pour onto the egg mixture, stirring constantly. Return to the saucepan and slowly heat, whisking until smooth and thick. Stir in the coconut. Cover with dampened greaseproof paper and leave until cold.

4. Spread the coconut filling in the pastry case. Whip the cream until holding soft peaks and spread over the top of the filling. Sprinkle over the toasted coconut and serve.

Index